Brittany Earns Her Ears

Brittany Earns Her Ears

My Secret Walt Disney World Cast Member Diary

EARNING YOUR EARS: VOLUME FIVE

Brittany DiCologero

Theme Park Press

Editor: Bob McLain
Layout: Artisanal Text

ISBN 978-1-941500-36-1
Printed in the United States of America

Theme Park Press | www.ThemeParkPress.com
Address queries to bob@themeparkpress.com

Contents

The quotes that begin each chapter are from Walt Disney.

About "Earning Your Ears"

The "Earning Your Ears" series chronicles the experiences of young people from around the country and around the world who leave home, often for the first time, to live and work in Walt Disney World or Disneyland for several months, or even longer.

They are given "roles" to perform, from working in a Disney restaurant or shop to donning a costume and becoming one of the Disney characters who appear in the parks.

Each book in the EARS series makes you an honorary cast member as the author takes you behind Disney's pixie dust curtain to learn things the Mouse would prefer you didn't know, and what no guidebook will tell you, including how the theme parks operate from the inside out and what Disney employees do when they're not wishing you a magical day.

The EARS series currently includes five books, with a new volume published by Theme Park Press every few months:

- Amber Earns Her Ears
- Ema Earns Her Ears
- Sara Earns Her Ears
- Katie Earns Her Ears
- Brittany Earns Her Ears

If you've ever wondered what it would be like not just to visit a Disney theme park but to work in one, the "Earning Your Ears" series is your E-ticket!

To learn about forthcoming books and everything there is to know about the Disney College Program, please visit us on Facebook:

Facebook.com/EarningYourEars

Foreword

I love publishing EARS books.

When I started the "Earning Yours Ears" series back in 2013, with *Amber Earns Her Ears*, I figured it would be a one-and-done. But Amber's book was not only popular, it was inspirational, too. Others who had taken (or were taking) the Disney College Program wanted to share their experiences.

Not everyone, unfortunately, can write an EARS book. For every twenty pitches I receive, one makes the grade. What amazes me is the diversity: no two stories are alike. And what amazes me even more is the hope and the wonder and the potential that each Disney College Program participant brings. Forget about the cynical accusations that Disney uses college program participants as low-wage labor. There's more to it.

Brittany DiCologero, the author of this book, was accepted into the DCP in 2011, but for various reasons, as you'll soon learn, she had to turn down the offer. She applied again in 2014. Once more, she was accepted—and this time she took it, even though she would be a college graduate by the time her program started.

Brittany didn't get her first choice of role. She didn't get her second choice, either. She got what many consider to be the absolute worst role in the absolute worst area of any Disney theme park. You'll soon find out how she handled it. You'll also learn more about the real, nitty-gritty inner workings of Disney than I've published in any EARS book, to date. When you finish *Brittany Earns Her Ears*, you'll almost be ready to work at Disney World yourself.

I publish EARS books because it feels good to publish EARS books. I don't sell a huge number of them. They do well, but the authors aren't relaxing on yachts. Most have gone on from their Disney experience to the real world of making grades in college and worrying about what kind of job awaits them and whether they'll be earning enough for a mortgage and what they really want to do with their lives.

For a few months, however, none of that matters. They're making minimum wage for menial labor in a sea of others doing the same thing. And they love it. It's their childhood dream come true. Whatever role Disney had played in their lives, they are now part of it. In Brittany's case, she has graduated from college and should be starting her career or pursuing a master's degree, but instead she's running the games in DinoLand. Like Amber and all the rest, she's on stage, as Disney likes to describe it, and making the same kind of magic that once was made for her.

So why, really, do I love publishing EARS books? If you read enough of them, you'll find life itself encapsulated: the uncertainty of whether you're good enough to make the cut, the transition from what you've known all your life to something new and quite grand, the settling in to work and friends and routine, the responsibility of being on your own and having others rely upon you, and finally, inevitably the winding down and the departure. All of this, in just a few months.

I could publish 100 EARS books and still not run out of unique tales about the Disney College Program.

Brittany's story is one of them.

Bob McLain
Theme Park Press
April 2, 2015

Introduction

All the adversity I've had in my life, all my troubles, and obstacles, have strengthened me... You may not realize it when it happens, but a kick in the teeth may be the best thing in the world for you.

"Hello?" ... "Hello? Can you still hear me?"

I paced back and forth in the narrow space between my roommate's bed and my own. I felt as though I had waited for this phone call for years, and now it was over. Throughout high school, and the first half of college, I waited for the day that I would receive the call to take my Disney College Program phone interview. In that moment however, all that was coming through the phone was silence.

-Click-

I looked down at my pink BlackBerry Curve nervously, reaffirming the obvious—that my call had been lost. I was about five minutes into the interview that would determine my acceptance, or lack thereof, into the Disney College Program...and the call was lost. Trying my best to remain calm, I stared intently at my cell phone hoping that it would ring again, preferably with that 407 area code. After what seemed like the most nerve-racking two minutes of my life, it finally rang.

"Hello?!" I answered on the first ring.

"Hi, Brittany?" questioned the voice on the other end, "It's Michelle from Disney College Program Recruiting. It would appear that our call was lost; we can continue with your interview now if you'd like."

I sighed a breath of relief, and the interview continued.

I do not remember the exact moment when I first learned about the Disney College Program. I have been obsessed with all things Disney for as long as I can remember, so eventually working for the company has always been in the back of my mind. The first time I visited Walt Disney World, I was three years old. Needless to say, I do not remember this trip, but it was only the beginning. I have vacationed there with my family most years since then, and have seriously considered participating in the college program since my freshman year of high school.

My initial plan for working for Disney was to participate in the CareerStart Program. CareerStart was similar to the College Program, but it was offered for recent high school graduates rather than college students. (CareerStart was discontinued in 2010.) When I was in high school, and still looking at colleges, I initially wanted to major in hospitality and tourism. Whether or not I would be working for the Walt Disney Company at a theme park, I knew I wanted to make a career in the tourism industry, so becoming a hospitality and tourism major in college seemed like a step in the right direction.

When it came time to choose a college and apply for Disney's CareerStart Program, my plan for working for Disney after high school, and for majoring in hospitality and tourism, began to fall apart. Of the colleges that had offered me scholarships, none of them had hospitality and tourism as a major. There were some that offered it as minors, as certificate programs, or as the concentration of a business major, but that was the closest I was going to get. I was not entirely heartbroken, as a business major seemed similar, at least in that I would learn transferable skills for both fields. As for the CareerStart Program, I tried hard to convince my family to see it as a good idea, but they never came around. My parents did not approve of me taking time off between high school and college, and with that, CareerStart was out of the picture. With both CareerStart and a hospitality and tourism major pushed aside, I enrolled as a business major at Saint Anselm College, a small, Catholic, liberal arts college in Manchester, New Hampshire, in the fall of 2010.

My time as a business major was short—only one semester. The only business class I took within the major was microeconomics, and I dreaded every second of it. The professor was great, and the workload was what I would have expected from any college course, but the subject matter did not interest me at all. My professor required us to read the *Wall Street Journal*, check Yahoo! Finance, and keep up with the stock market—all things he said we'd be doing for the rest of our lives in the business field. I struggled to find anything interesting on Yahoo! Finance, and the stock market bored me nearly to death. I could not imagine myself getting into the habit of reading the *Wall Street Journal* for the rest of my life. What I did enjoy about my microeconomics class was the mention of historical, yet business-related events. If my professor asked us to graph supply and demand, I would be clueless, but if he asked us about the Great Depression, or colonial mercantilism, I would have been all over it.

My adviser was just about to fill out my paperwork to register me for a second semester of business classes, when I blurted, "I think I want to change my major."

I expected her to be surprised, and perhaps even disappointed, that I wanted to get myself out of the business department, but it actually seemed as though she knew I didn't belong there herself. When she asked what major responded, I wasn't very helpful: "I don't know, maybe history?"

Rather than telling me to keep my business major and also take a history class to see how I liked it, she handed me a change of major form and sent me upstairs to the History Department, where a professor (who would soon be my new adviser) enrolled me in the only available history class that would fit into my freshman schedule. And the rest, as they say, was history.

As a sophomore at Saint A's, I watched my friends apply for study abroad programs and faraway (and often unpaid) internships. I hoped to find a paid internship at a museum for the summer, but that was many months away. While browsing one of the Disney fan websites I frequented, I saw a post about the Disney College Program. The thought of participating in the program was still in the back of my mind, but after my family's disapproval of CareerStart, I did not expect that applying for the College Program would go much better.

Then I noticed that applications for the Spring 2012 program were already out. Before discussing the idea with anyone else, I submitted an application. One hour later, I received a confirmation email from Disney Recruiting. Another hour passed and I received an email inviting me to take the Web-Based Interview. I had no idea that the process would be moving along this quickly. I planned on going to Career Services and my adviser's office to make appointments to meet with them and discuss participating in the program, and now I was already invited to take the first interview. During my break from classes that day, I settled down in my school's dining hall to take the Web-Based Interview. I felt fairly confident after completing the online portion of the interview process, but I still did not want to get my hopes up—not only because I didn't know if I would be offered a phone interview, but because I had yet to set up appointments with Career Services and my adviser to "okay" the program in the first place.

By 3:30 that afternoon, an invitation for the phone interview was in my inbox. While I was extremely excited, I also panicked, as I needed to head to Staples, where I worked as a sales associate, right after class, and would therefore put off making those appointments until the following day. I scheduled my phone interview for exactly one week from then, at 10:15 am.

The following day, when I tried to make appointment with my adviser and Career Services, I found that the earliest openings would be *after* the phone interview with Disney. I did not like this situation at all, but there was nothing I could do about it. My weekdays were spent in class and my weeknights were spent at Staples. I needed to arrange a day where I could get to work late if I wanted to have time to squeeze a meeting in between my 1:30-3:00 class and 4:00-9:30 shift at Staples. I was worried that I'd successfully complete Disney's application process only to be told by the college that I wouldn't be able to take time off for it.

The day of my phone interview came, after a very long, anxious week, full of waiting and stalking the Disney College Program Spring/ Spring Advantage 2012 Facebook page. This was my first phone interview, so I did not know what to expect. I jotted down some notes, though nothing too extensive, and made sure the door to my dorm room was shut tight, and all was quiet in my building. I debated on completing the interview in my car, because it would be impossible to control an entire building full of college students noise-wise, but thankfully my room proved to be very quiet that morning.

At 10:00 am, my phone began to vibrate and a phone number with a 407 area code appeared on the screen. I answered the phone nervously, and the interview began. The interviewer I had was friendly and professional. At the start of the interview, she went over what to do if the call was lost. She said that if for any reason we lost connection, she would call back and the interview would continue. As soon as she mentioned this, I became nervous as I realized that this could very well happen. The reception in the area near my building was not the best, as I knew all too well from the number of times calls with my family had been lost from my room. I began regretting the decision to stay in my building rather than my car, and I thought about how weird it would be to wander out to my car mid-interview.

I decided that staying put would be best, so I made myself comfortable atop my lofted bed and placed my notes in front of me as the interviewer went over some basic information from my application. She confirmed that I was only applying to the Florida program and not California, as well as the Advantage program being my first choice, with regular Spring as my second. (The Advantage program lasts about two months longer than the regular program.) The first couple of questions she asked were yes-or-no, though I was able to elaborate my answers a little bit. She asked if I had read the guidelines for the Disney Look, which I had. This question was followed with confirmations that I understood that my hair would be returning to its natural color, and that I thankfully had no tattoos to cover up. She also confirmed that I would be receptive to working outside regardless of the weather, and that I was comfortable living with roommates. After these preliminary Q&A's, she proceeded to the actual interview questions.

"What made you want to apply to th—"

-Silence-

"Hello?" … "Hello? Can you still hear me?"

And this was how my call was lost, for my first interview with the Disney College Program. Right when we were about to start discussing why I wanted to apply for the internship, BOOM—gone. To say this was stressful is an understatement. Even though I was told at the start of the interview what to do if the call was lost, I still panicked. This was such an important moment to me, and it was either over entirely or at least disrupted before it had even started. When the interviewer called back, which was only about one or two minutes after connection was lost, she was very calm and hardly mentioned that the lost connection even happened. I assume she gives tons of interviews and this was a fairly regular occurrenceso she was probably not even phased by it. But I had become nervous, and felt the butterflies fluttering in my stomach.

"What made you want to apply for the Disney College Program?"

As I answered the question I immediately heard the sound of typing coming through the phone. I know that most employers take notes on prospective employees, but the sound of the keyboard was particularly anxiety-inducing to me—especially when the interviewer would say things like, "Alright, great. Just give me one moment to make sure I record all of that." I became less nervous and more comfortable as the interview went on. While the questions in the interview were not necessarily easy, the tone and personality of the recruiter made me feel more at ease than I usually did at interviews. I also had the luxury of glancing down at my notes if necessary, since the interview was done over the phone.

"Can you describe a time at your current job when you had to multi-task?"

I remember thinking that I should have come up with a better answer for this question. I did not prepare for this one in particular, so I answered more candidly than I did with some of the others. I explained to the interviewer that while I worked at the Customer Service desk at Staples you could be looking up a customer's rewards information while helping someone on the phone and being asked questions by other customers near the desk. I stated that the customer comes first, and even though three different customers could be vying for your attention at the same time, multi-tasking is a necessity because each customer needs to feel as though you are giving him your full attention. If giving so many customers your full attention was simply impossible, I mentioned that I would do my best to find other available associates to assist me. Another scenario I gave was that if you have a task of restocking a shelf and a customer asks where an item is, you should stop what you are doing and walk the customer to the product, ask if they need help with anything else, and only then go back to your task. I felt that both of these scenarios were pretty common sense to anyone who has worked in retail, but the question caught me off guard.

"What would you do if a guest spills a drink near where you are working?"

"Do you prefer working in a fast-paced work environment or a slow-paced work environment?"

"Can you describe a stressful situation you've experienced at a job and how you handled it?"

"Why do you want to work at the Walt Disney World Resort?"

This was by far the most important question of the interview. My advice to any prospective applicants reading this book would be to spend most of your time preparing an answer. When you hear someone say that you need to smile through the phone, and you think that's weird, it's not. Okay, well it is, it's really weird to smile freakishly to yourself while you're alone taking a phone interview. But it helped me, and it'll help you, too. You'll understand it when you get there, just like I did.

I answered this question with something like the following:

> I want to work at the Walt Disney World Resort primarily so that I can bring magic to guests. When I visit the resort as a guest, magic is created for me thanks to the Cast Members who work there, and I want to be the person to bring that magic to others. Even simple things like saying 'Welcome home' when you enter a Disney resort or 'Have a magical day' when you purchase something in a gift shop go a long way in creating the magic that is unique to Disney vs. other vacation destinations. I'm extremely interested in the guest services field, and Disney is, in my opinion, the best company to receive training for this. Though my current job at Staples is in customer service, there is only so much I can do to create a 'magical' shopping experience for a guest. I feel that through working at the Walt Disney World Resort, I would reach my full potential in terms of guest service, and I would really just love the opportunity to bring a magical moment to someone else's day who is visiting the resort as a guest.

> Like I've already hinted at, I would also love to be able to say that I interned for the Walt Disney Company. Having the Disney name on my resume would help me out a great deal when I graduate and am looking for full-time work. Many employers associate the company with excellent training and values, and I feel that in the work force this would give me an edge over other applicants.

After this mini-speech, my interviewer asked if I had any questions, which I did not. At the time I really felt as though I should have, as I know that it looks better when you ask questions during job interviews, but anything that I would have asked was already answered for me. She then told me that I would be notified of their decision in a couple of weeks, and that was it. The phone interview was over. Not including the couple of minutes where the call was lost, my entire interview took about 25 minutes.

Following the interview, I felt oddly confident. There were a couple of times during the interview where I questioned my responses, but the recruiter made the whole experience very comfortable, so I felt good about it. The nervousness remained, however, because I did not know how my school would handle the program if I were to be accepted, and I would not know for another three days, when my appointments were scheduled. Two days after my phone interview, I saw an email from Disney recruiting on my cell phone. When I saw the "Congratulations!" in the subject header of the email, I dropped my phone in shock—I had been accepted into the Disney College Program.

I followed the instructions in the email and printed out the complete information they had sent me regarding my acceptance. I was accepted for Spring Advantage, and my role was to be Merchandise. The strange thing about being accepted was that I was so excited, but at the same time I felt like I couldn't even tell anyone. I told my roommate, because I shared a dorm room with her and wouldn't have been able to contain my excitement. I told my parents, though as expected, their enthusiasm was nowhere close to mine. I told a couple of my close friends and my boyfriend, but that was it. I was worried about telling too many people in case it turned out that I could not accept the offer. This put a damper on the excitement of being accepted.

The next day I met with my adviser to discuss the program. He had never heard of it, so most of our time together was spent with him gathering information from the official Disney College Program web site. He knew that our school did not recognize the program as an internship, and I would have to be taking some kind of classes while down there or over the summer if I did not want to fall behind. We then looked through some of the classes that Disney offered and realized that none would be useful for my history major, but if I was serious about the program, I might be able to receive some sort of business credits, instead. So far, so good. I didn't mind receiving some extra credit for business classes; I used to be a Business major, after all. Before leaving my adviser's office, he reminded me to check with Career Services and Financial Aid, because if the program was not recognized by my school I might have to un-enroll from college and take a leave of absence.

My meeting with the Career Services woman was not much different. She pointed out that the program was not recognized as an internship, so I would not receive any credit unless I took extra classes to make up for it. She also told me what I was most worried about hearing—because the program was not recognized by the school, I would have to take a leave of absence. A leave of absence might mean losing scholarship money. On to the Financial Aid Office I went.

I will always remember the Financial Aid Office as the place where I found out that I could not participate in the Disney College Program Spring 2012 season, *even though I could have theoretically taken summer classes, and I was already accepted.* The terms of my scholarship clearly stated that I could not take a leave of absence during my enrollment at Saint Anselm. A leave of absence would have voided my scholarship, and without my scholarship I would not have been able to afford Saint A's.

So that was it. After the emotional rush of applying for the program on a whim, the whole experience was over before it began. Logging onto my Disney dashboard and declining the offer was extremely difficult. I made a post on the Disney College Program's Facebook page explaining my situation and wishing the other hopefuls the best of luck, and for a while I simply moved on with my life.

For about a year, I was able to block out most memories and desires for the Disney College Program. I did find a new job over the summer of 2012 working at a small museum on the Freedom Trail in Boston. Rather than getting my hopes up *again* about working for Disney, I began looking for internships in my field, and seriously thinking about graduate school. The more I talked to others who had done the program, though, the more I wanted to do it. It took until my junior year for the facts of declining the offer to really sink in. I felt gipped that I was unable to do the program because of my school not recognizing it. Having to decline the offer was not my fault. I had it all figured out: I would take summer classes and still graduate on time. There was no good reason why I should have had to decline the offer.

I did end up completing internships in my field, working in collections management, as a researcher at historic sites and museums, and even for a historic district commission where I researched and wrote a tour of an old cemetery. Although I could see myself turning any of these jobs into a career, I still had a strong desire to work for Disney. I felt cheated out of it

After months of debating and going back and forth about what to do after I graduate, I finally came to a conclusion. I would apply for the Disney College Program again, for Fall 2014. This would be my last possible opportunity to complete the program, and I knew that if I were to give up without trying, I would live to regret it.

Chapter One

I always like to look on the optimistic side of life, but I am
realistic enough to know that life is a complex matter.

Applications for the Fall 2014 program were expected out in early February. In preparation for the application, I've done a substantial amount of research that I had never really got around to doing the last time I applied. In 2011, I leisurely researched the program. If I happened to be on some kind of Disney website and it was mentioned, I would read on, but I never actively searched for information. This season is different. I have been borderline obsessive trying to learn everything I possibly can about the program.

One website that has always been a huge part of my Disney obsession is WDWmagic.com. The college program section of the forum is relatively small compared to those on other sites, but the website as a whole is very helpful. Another website well known among Disney fans is Disboards.com. I am more of a lurker on Disboards and I only visit there occasionally. (A "lurker" is someone who reads messages on internet forums but seldom or never posts.)

Don't overlook YouTube. Many former participants have made "vlogs", or video blogs, during their programs, and I find these to be very helpful. In addition, Tumblr and Blogger host a number of useful blogs produced by former program participants. The best way to find these blogs is to Google "Disney College Program blogs". You'll come across one that you find interesting, and chances are that person will link to another person's blog, and so on and so forth. I know lots of people are very into Tumblr, and that you can follow certain accounts to receive updates from them. I assume many people are lurkers when it comes to following blogs, as my own blog, destinationdisneyworld. blogspot.com, has a high number of views, but few followers.

The only physical book I have read about the College Program has been *Amber Earns her Ears*, from Theme Park Press, the first book in this series (which is now up to five books, with mine the fifth!). Amber's book follows her journey on the now defunct Career Start Program and then the College Program itself.

This time around, the Disney College Program Fall/Fall Advantage 2014 Facebook group was also relatively helpful. I say "relatively" because I'm a firm believer that anything read on Facebook should be taken with a grain of salt. There are groups like this for every program and season, and many participants use them as a way to find their roommates. If you've been in a Facebook group for your college prior to your arrival freshman year, you've had a similar experience. The groups are great because many program participants have done the program one or more times, so they are available to offer advice. Many times, the admins of the groups are alumni, or sometimes even full- or part-time Cast Members. Because these groups include so many members who have experienced the program first-hand, it is easy to send a message to someone if you have questions about anything.

At the same time, however, these groups will also have lots of members who know much less than you do about the program. This means that there will be lots of repetitive questions, and sometimes rumors. I don't mean rumors in the middle-school sort of way; the rumors on these Facebook groups are more like "accidental rumors". Sometimes, applicants are misinformed, and because they do not realize that they are misinformed, they post what they believe to be correct information. I do not believe that they are intentionally trying to cause confusion, but there are always instances where things posted on the Facebook groups are simply just not true. The "accidental rumors" I see posted on Disney College Program Facebook groups often involve things like what discounts participants receive, and how many students apply for each program vs. how many are actually accepted. These are perfect examples of rumors that were started with good intentions—discounts may have changed since the person posting last heard, and numbers of applicants thrown out by recruiters are often estimates, so there will not be one set figure. Regardless, I think that the Facebook group is a great way to get to know other potential participants before the program starts, especially as it gives you the ability to communicate with alumni, as long as you can sift through the unnecessary information and accidental rumors.

I always assumed that I would find my roommates on the Facebook group, but I never imagined that I would find them so quickly. About one month before applications were expected to come out, I already had two roommates. I bonded with Holly and Kaitie through the Facebook group because of our similar interests (wine and cats). The three of us have all been accepted into the program before—I'm actually the only one who was not an alum. We were all worried about finding roommates before applications even came out, but we get along well and knew we would like to live together if we are all accepted.

One of the other ways that I have been preparing for applications has been through revisions of my resume. A resume is not necessary for the Disney College Program, but the application form asks for all of the information that a resume would contain. Because I may also apply for professional internships at some point, revising my resume is a must.

I currently work at a museum and historic site on Boston's Freedom Trail, and while it is much smaller than anything on Disney's property, it is a tourist destination—meaning our visitors are similar to the kind of guests that visit Walt Disney World. While Disney-speak dictates that visitors are referred to as guests, they are also technically tourists as they are travelling to a specific destination for the purpose of vacationing or entertainment. A tourist is a very specific type of customer, and I feel as though my work on the Freedom Trail can be applied to work in the program, and would be beneficial if I were to make it to the phone interview. Someone visiting Boston on vacation is not entirely different from someone visiting Walt Disney World. A tourist in Boston will often ask for directions, things to do, and places to eat. Tourists are on vacation, and they want the best experience they can possibly have. After paying potentially thousands of dollars for airfare and hotel rooms, they want to make sure that their trip to Boston is extremely enjoyable—just like a Disney guest.

Perhaps unfortunately, I am a realist. This means that while most of my time has been spent reading up on what it's like to work for Disney, I am always thinking of the possibility that it will not work out. With rumors of the application process becoming increasingly difficult, I cannot bring myself to ignore that I may not be accepted. The realist in me is not allowing my hopes to go too far up, especially before applications even come out. I've also seriously thought about the timeline of my previous application: the entire process, from the submission of the application to my acceptance, only took about one week. This is not common, as I've read numerous accounts of applicants waiting weeks to hear back about any part of their applications. I can't expect a quick acceptance again; if I get one at all. The next few weeks or months are going to be tough.

The 2014 application season has yet another difficulty that the 2012 season lacked. My boyfriend, Chaz, is also applying for the program, which presents us with the possibility that only one of us may be accepted. This will be the first time that Chaz applies for any kind of job with Disney. He's also a huge Disney nerd like me. He is equally as obsessed with Disneyland as I am with Disney World. We find ourselves having arguments fairly often over things like which parade is superior, Spectromagic (R.I.P.) or the Main Street Electrical Parade.

The most difficult part about applying for the DCP with your significant other is the reality that only one of you will be accepted. We've discussed what we would do if this were to happen, though I'm optimistic that we will either both be accepted or both be denied. We have agreed that if only one of us gets in, the other would not stand in the way.

Chapter Two

We keep moving forward, opening new doors, and doing new things,
because we're curious and curiosity keeps leading us down new paths.

Applications for the Fall/Fall Advantage 2014 Disney College Program
went live on February 6, 2014. For a day that should have been
very climactic, with all of the energy and anxiety leading up to it,
I remained relatively calm, and sort of zoned out. I had been going
back and forth between the twin bed of my dorm room and Health
Services all week, so as much as I would have loved to focus on applications, they were not a priority. As it turned out, I had a chest cold,
which Health Services wanted to monitor in case it turned into bron-
chitis or tonsillitis. When I returned from my second trip to Health
Services that day, I logged onto Facebook and saw that applications
had indeed opened up.

I was feverish and hopped up on cold medicine, and would have
liked to be in a better frame of mind when completing the application. I immediately thought about Chaz—we had discussed what we
would do when the applications came out, and we ultimately decided
that we would apply at the same time. (We would not be together,
though, as I was at school in New Hampshire and he was home, in
Massachusetts.) I texted him to let him know that applications were
out and that we should apply. Chaz was still at work, so we agreed
that we would submit the application at the same time when he got
home that evening.

A couple of hours went by, and Chaz still wasn't home from work.
I spent my time in bed, scanning the Facebook group and checking
my email, since my fever wasn't allowing me to concentrate on homework or sleeping. I noticed all of the excitement from others in the
Facebook group who had already submitted applications, and with the
girls I was planning on rooming with. One of these girls, Holly, had
already set up her phone interview before Chaz and I even applied.
Chaz eventually let me know that he was running late. I wanted to

wait for Chaz, I really did...but...I'm impatient. I couldn't bear to read everyone else's comments about scheduling phone interviews. I submitted my application about an hour before Chaz got home from work.

The application itself was almost exactly as I remembered it from the last time I applied in 2011. The questions were similar to those on any entry level job application. It didn't take me long to complete it, because I already had an account set up on Disney's career website. (Once you set up an account on the website most of your information is saved, so a lot of the application was already completed for me.) Just like the last time I applied, the most interesting part of the application was the role selection portion. Unlike last time, however, I put a great deal of thought into which roles I would like. When I applied in 2011, I had done hardly any research on the program. This time I wanted to be prepared to rank each of the roles according to my actual interest in them:

- High Interest: Merchandise, Attractions, Main Entrance Operations, Recreation, Full Service Food and Beverage, Vacation Planner.
- Moderate Interest: Quick Service Food and Beverage, PhotoPass, Hospitality, Hopper, Bell Services Dispatch/Greeter, Costuming, Character Attendant, Bibbidi Bobbidi Boutique/Pirates League, Concierge, Transportation.
- Low Interest: Custodial, Housekeeping.
- No Interest: Lifeguard, Character Performer.

As of the Spring 2014 recruiting season, not every applicant is invited to take a Web-Based Interview (WBI.) The last time I applied, everyone was able to take the WBI, and applicants would be denied if they failed that or did not have a good phone interview. Now, applicants can be rejected from their applications alone. There was some talk on the Facebook group that the process of selecting which applicants would receive the WBI was random, but this is not the case. As the writers of the official DCP blog have pointed out, the process is not random, but rather some applicants are not asked to move on due to the information in their applications.

After I submitted my application, I joined a conversation on Facebook with my (hopefully) future roommates. Among the three of us who definitely wanted to live together (Holly, Kaitie, and I), Holly already had her phone interview scheduled, and Kaitie was still waiting for her invitation to take the WBI. Within a few minutes, Kaitie had received her invitation and Chaz had gotten home from work. I sat in front of my laptop, still feverish on the bed in my dorm room, while Kaitie completed her WBI and Chaz created a profile on the website. During this time, I compulsively refreshed my Dashboard to see if the status of my application had changed. (The Dashboard is the tool on Disney's career website that displays the status of your applications as well as any upcoming interviews.) Initially, my Dashboard was blank, and I had not even received the "Thank you for applying" email. I assumed this was because so many people were trying to apply on the first day, but I was too feverish and delirious to care all that much.

"I didn't pass."

I stared down at a Facebook message that had suddenly popped up from Kaitie.

"If you're joking, that's not funny." I responded.

"I'm totally not joking right now," she typed, "I'm about to cry."

Kaitie did not pass her WBI. I had no idea what to say. I felt as though we had become such great friends over the past couple of months, so I was heartbroken that we would not be living together in Florida. I still questioned if she were actually serious, because for all I knew she could have been messing with me. I was hoping this was all a joke, and she actually passed but wanted to be "funny" and see if I would fall for it. A couple of minutes later, Holly messaged me asking if I'd heard what happened to Kaitie. She wasn't kidding. Kaitie, one of my "hopefully" future roommates, and an alumnus of the DCP, did not pass the WBI. She called Disney's recruiting department the next day to see if there was anything else she could do, since she had worked for the company before and therefore was obviously a good fit for the program. Unfortunately, she received the generic answer: "You failed the WBI, try again next season."

I had never been so nervous about the DCP. The first time I applied, I was accepted into the program within one week. The entire process back then was so much easier than I expected it to be, and I was in a state of shock that an alumnus would be cut so soon. To make matters worse, I felt as though Kaitie and I had become very good friends in the time leading up to applications going live, so it was difficult to imagine what she was going through. In addition to feeling bad for Kaitie, I also selfishly felt bad for myself because I lost a roommate before the application process had really even taken off.

Chaz informed me that he submitted his application a few minutes after Kaitie had told me the news about her WBI. He and Kaitie knew of each other and they spoke occasionally on the Facebook group. I didn't want to tell him what happened to Kaitie right away in fear of making him nervous since he had just begun the process. I was just about done with the stress of applications, and I was exhausted from not sleeping the night before due to my chest cold, so I planned on going to sleep after Chaz submitted his application. Of course, I checked my phone before going to bed, and I noticed an email from Disney College Program Recruiting:

> Dear Brittany,
>
> Thank you for your interest in the Disney College Program.
>
> Based on the information you provided in your application, you have been selected to participate in an initial interview for a possible opportunity with the Disney College Program.
>
> This initial interview is a Web-Based Interview. We ask you to complete this interview within three (3) days from receipt of this email. The Web-Based Interview can be accessed on any computer that has a high-speed Internet connection.
>
> At the end of the Web-Based Interview, you will be informed about whether or not you will continue in the interview process. Web-Based Interview results are valid for six (6) months.

I was in such a conflicted state emotionally upon reading this email. I was sweating due to my fever and fatigued to no end from my lack of sleep the previous night. Taking the WBI at that exact moment was the last thing I should do, as I just wanted to rest and get better so that I'd be able to go to work the following day. I also thought about Kaitie, and how terrible I felt being excited for receiving the invitation for the WBI when she had just failed hers. I told Chaz that I was offered the WBI, and he suggested that I wait until the morning and take it then, because I was obviously out of it that night from being sick. He was probably the more logical one between the two of us in this situation, but I knew I couldn't wait to take it. I knew that

I'd be up all night with my cold again, and the spectre of taking the WBI would have me tossing and turning even more. I clicked the link in the email and decided to take the WBI—fever, delirium, and all.

The WBI was almost the same as I remembered it. There were two sections, the first being questions with multiple choice answers and the second being a series of statements to which you answer Strongly Disagree / Disagree / Neutral / Agree / Strongly Agree. The entire interview is timed—50 seconds per question for the first section, and 20 seconds per question for the second section. To me, the timing is the most stressful part of the interview. Even more stressful is that there is no timer showing you how long you have left. I guess with either 50 or 20 seconds per question you don't really have time to look at a timer, but regardless I wish there was one. You also answer the questions one at a time and click "Next" after you complete each one. I know that some applicants do not like this setup, because it does not allow you to see how many questions you have left. You could be almost done, or you could be toward the beginning, and you would have no idea until you finish.

The questions in the first section contained some inquiries about why I chose the college I did, and a couple of situations for me to decipher. The questions about my college I found somewhat confusing because I was not quite sure what kind of answers Disney wanted. For example, "I chose my college to be close to my family," and you would respond with how true that statement was. I thought the answer to this could have gone either way. I could have answered that this was entirely true, because family is important and Disney obviously believes in family, too. At the same time, I thought making it seem like proximity to family was not a priority would be a good answer as well because it would show that you are independent and willing to move far away for the DCP. In the end, I chose mostly neutral answers for these questions.

This section also contained a question about whether or not I've lived in residence halls before. I know this is important for the DCP—after all, I'd be living in an apartment with roommates—but I do not remember this question being on the WBI before. I also think that if the answer they want is "Yes", they are putting some students at a serious, and perhaps unfair, disadvantage. Some students are commuters, and in many cases community colleges do not have residence halls, so those students have no choice but to be commuters.

Since I live on campus, neither of those situations apply to me, but I still thought it was a weird question to have in the WBI.

An example of the other kind of question on the first section of the WBI was, "A child is using a hammer and hits his thumb, what should you do?" *What kind of parent lets a child use a hammer?* But in all seriousness, this was a multiple choice question and I answered that I would take care of the child's thumb before doing anything else. I know that safety is the most prioritized of Disney's "Four Keys to a Great Guest Experience", so to me this was the obvious answer. What an odd scenario, though! Last time I believe this question had a more realistic scenario, like a child scraping a knee or spilling a drink.

I found the second section of the interview to be much easier. These questions were a series of statements in which you respond with how much you agree or disagree. The statements here are largely about your ability to provide top-notch guest service, and your personality in general. The key to success is to remain consistent in your answers, and to stick with Strongly Agree / Strongly Disagree rather than the other choices. Many statements are repeated with different wording, so it is important to pay close attention to everything you read. You're being assessed on how you would act as a Disney employee, with such things as whether you feel the customer is always being right, whether you have a positive personality, and whether you are always on time for work. *I am always on time for work. Of course I am! Why would I disagree with this statement even if I wasn't?!* The nice part about the WBI, unlike the rest of the application process, is that you receive the results immediately, and there is no waiting involved. I passed and was invited to schedule a phone interview.

My passing the WBI was bittersweet. I was still upset about Kaitie, and I did not want to post all over Facebook that I was moving on to the phone interview. I told Chaz and Holly, and called my parents, but the rest of Facebook did not need to know right away. I could not imagine the way that Kaitie was feeling as she watched the people she'd grown close to move on with the process while she was left behind, and I did not want to shove my achievement in her face. I was also in a delusional, anxious frame of mind at this point, and I was seriously ready for bed. I scheduled my phone interview for a week from that day, assuming that I would be feeling better by then. Before going to bed, I asked Chaz to check his email and Dashboard. I assumed that since we applied at about the same time, he probably also had an invitation for the WBI and just didn't realize it yet. His dashboard still read "Submission", while mine read "In Progress".

The next day, Chaz checked his Dashboard hourly, hoping that his status would change and he would be invited to take the WBI. All day—nothing. Reality once again began to sink in: There was a chance only one of us would get into the program. I kept telling myself that it was too early in the process to worry over this, and what was most important was for me to prepare for my phone interview the following week. Applying for the DCP with your significant other is much more difficult than I had imagined it to be. There is a huge difference between saying it's okay if only one of you gets accepted, and it actually *being* okay if only one of you gets accepted.

Chapter Three

*Why worry? If you've done the very best you
can, worrying won't make it any better.*

Valentine's Day, 2014. My phone interview for the Disney College Program was scheduled for 7:45 pm on that Friday night. Fifteen minutes before my interview was to begin, I told my family that I needed absolute silence and locked myself in my room. I also taped a sign to the door reminding them that I was not to be interrupted.

To be technical, my phone interview actually began at 7:59 PM. (The invitation for the phone interview explicitly states that the interviewer may call up to fifteen minutes prior or fifteen minutes after the time that your interview is scheduled for.) This meant that for nearly half an hour, I was huddled on the floor of my room, staring at the notes I'd made. I wore Mickey Mouse slippers and had my Oswald stuffed animal next to me, as well as my acceptance letter from the first time I applied just for good measure. From what I recall of my first DCP phone interview back in 2011, my phone rang right on time, but my 2014 phone call came almost a full fifteen minutes late.

Not surprisingly, the interview was similar to the one I had in 2011. After the recruiter got through the preliminary stuff, such as confirming the information that I'd put on my application and asking some standard employment eligibility questions, she asked how I'd hold up in the hot, humid, sometimes rainy Florida climate. Just fine, I told her, and then she got down to business: "Why do you want to participate in the Disney College Program?" My answer wasn't much changed from last time. If it worked then, it should work now, too.

I was then asked to describe the duties at my current job. I stumbled a bit, since at the time I had three part-time jobs, and didn't want to confuse her or talk too much. I focused on my work work at the museum and historic site on Boston's Freedom Trail, which I subtly compared to Disney, and that seemed to impress her.

I was also asked standard questions like "Do you prefer working as an individual or as part of a team?" "Do you prefer a fast paced or a slow paced work environment?" "How would you remain calm in an emergency situation?" "How would you go about completing your task if you are interrupted?" "How would you deal with a job that can be repetitive?" None of them surprised me, and I gave the answers that I knew Disney wanted to hear.

Following these questions, the recruiter read off the roles that I had expressed interest in on my application, and made sure that I was still receptive to those areas. She asked for my top three role choices, and I told her Vacation Planner, Merchandise, and Attractions. She described these roles and asked me specific questions about them, such as whether I thought my current job skills would be transferable to the skills required to be a Vacation Planner (in other words, the person who works in the ticket booths at the front of the parks). I told her that selling extended warranties at Staples, where I also worked, was comparable to selling tickets at Disney World.

The recruiter then did the standard spiel about the Disney Look, confirming that I had no visible tattoos or piercings, and asked whether I'd be comfortable living with roommates. *Of course, I would!* From there the interview began to wind down, and I was asked if I had any questions. This time, I did. I wanted to know whether my chances for acceptance would be affected because I had turned down Disney's offer in 2011. No, she said, it wouldn't.

And with that, it was all over. Now there was nothing left to do but wait.

Initially, I felt happy and confident; the interview had gone well, and I was optimistic that I'd be accepted right away, just like last time. But soon I began to overthink my answers. Had I said too much? Too little? Had I sounded nervous? Had I forgotten to smile? I went from hoping for a quick acceptance to hoping for any acceptance at all.

My other "regret", if you can even call it that, was that I did not request any specific work locations during the interview. In my first interview, I was asked where at Disney World I'd most like to work, but this time I wasn't asked that question. I didn't even notice until the interview was over. Maybe it's best that I didn't bring it up, since it's possible that the more things you ask for, and the more particular you are about what you want to do in the Disney College Program, the more Disney will accept instead someone who is just happy to be there, anywhere.

Now that my application process is over, the waiting game begins—not only for myself, but for Holly, my potential roommate, and for Chaz. Holly had her phone interview a few days before me. Chaz is still in the Submission stage of the application process. He is very proud of me for making it to the phone interview, but we are both anxiously awaiting his invitation to take the WBI.

While the waiting game is the worst part of applying for the DCP, I am happy that the application process is over. I have to take a comprehensive exam to graduate from college, and without the stress of the DCP application, I will be able to focus most of my time and energy on preparing for that exam. Worrying will not make the wait any easier, so I am perfectly content to focus on school until I receive an email with Disney's decision.

Chapter Four

All our dreams can come true if we have the courage to pursue them.

In the week following my phone interview, I saw on the Facebook page that applicants were already being accepted. Phone interviews started on February 9, and mine was not until the 14th, so at first I was not too worried that I hadn't heard back yet. In applying for jobs with Disney, most applicants believe: "No news is good news." But, while scrolling through the posts on the Facebook page, I began to realize that some of the phone interview dates for those being accepted were either on the 14th or after it. I tried not to stress out.

Within the next week my roommate-to-be Holly, was accepted, as were two other girls we knew in the Facebook group. After things fell through with Kaitie, there was talk that we would room with these girls, but it did not work out. Both of them were accepted that week, so out of my little group of friends, I was the only one left waiting.

I was getting impatient. I could not help but compare the 2014 season, with me left hanging, to the 2011 season, with me accepted right away. By March 1, I had made the decision to only check my email and Dashboard once a day, for my own sanity. I realized that I had been bringing my phone with me everywhere, and my obsession with checking my email was becoming too much.

That morning my mom was making breakfast, and I was moping at the kitchen table because I hadn't received my email yet.

"It's going to come today," my mom said, as I placed my phone on the chair next to me so I wouldn't constantly keep checking it.

"I'm not going to get my hopes up."

"It will come within the next hour or so. Definitely by noon."

"That's not funny," I told her. "If you get that in my head, and then it doesn't come today, I'm going to go even crazier than I already have."

Approximately thirty minutes later, I was just about to turn my phone off for the day when I decided to check my email one more time—and immediately threw my phone down on the table, speechless. I could see an email from Disney College Recruiting, with the subject line "Congratulations!" Somehow, my mom had predicted the time of my acceptance down to the hour—which was good for her, because she would have never heard the end of it if she had guessed wrong. I was shaking and hesitant to click the link in the email to see which position I had been offered. My mom kept reassuring me, telling me that she knew I would be accepted, though her reassurance quickly turned to excitement over which role I had been offered. Of course, the webpage with the offer details that would include my role description seemed to take forever to load, and then it told me I'd entered the wrong password. For a moment, I couldn't remember the right password!

When I was finally able to read the offer letter, I learned that my role was Merchandise and that my hourly wage would be $7.93. Being offered a position in Merchandise was somewhat surprising. Vacation Planner had been my first choice, and most of the questions I was asked during my phone interview had focused on this role. I had assumed that either I would be accepted for Vacation Planner or I would receive an NLIC (No Longer In Consideration) email. My second choice, and the second most talked-about role in my phone interview was Attractions. To be fair, there is really no reason why I should have been offered a position in Attractions, as I had no experience in this area. Merchandise was my third choice, and I was not asked any questions about this role at all, probably because my work experience led the interviewer to conclude that I was most qualified for Merchandise, and that's what I'd be offered.

While I was surprised, it wasn't a complete shock—and it was certainly not a disappointment. Even though it was not my first choice, I was still extremely excited to become a Merchandise Cast Member in August. I had worked at Staples as a cashier for four years, and have had some retail experience in every job I've held since then. Retail has a bad reputation as a line of work, but like any job it really is what you make of it. One of the things that I am looking forward to most in this role is that I have heard that it is very easy to pick up shifts at different locations. In Merchandise, unlike in other roles, such as Attractions, most of the required training is generic, so Cast Members in this role can work at many different locations.

The offer letter also had details about the Disney Look, or standards of appearance that Disney enforces for Cast Members working onstage (aka in the public view). Following the guidelines outlined in the Disney Look is critical to working as a Cast Member, and the only way to "get out" of the Disney Look would be if you needed a medical or religious accommodation.

Some of what the Disney Look entails is similar to employee guidelines for most jobs that involve working with the public. For instance, Disney prohibits all Cast Members from doing things like eating and smoking while onstage. The Disney Look guidelines also make note that Disney is a first-name company, which means that name tags must be worn at all times. Disney's nametags must contain the Cast Member's first name (or middle name/appropriate nickname) as well as his or her college or hometown. If the Cast Member speaks more than one language fluently, language pins may be added to the nametag as well. Not surprisingly, the Disney Look prohibits visible body modifications like tattoos and piercings; the key word is *visible*—Disney doesn't care if you have lots of tattoos or piercings, as long as you keep them hidden.

After double-checking to be sure I wouldn't run afoul of the Disney Look, I sent Disney the $304.50 in fees they required to formally place me in the program. Among other things, the fees would cover my first month's rent in the Disney apartment I'd be sharing with my roommates. then I faced the tricky task of selecting an arrival date. Holly had chosen August 4 as her arrival date, and I had no choice but to chooe that date as well-otherwise, we might not end up in the same apartment, since Disney requires roommates to arrive on the same day.

Later in the afternoon on March 1, I made a Facebook status announcing my acceptance into the Disney College Program. The next couple of days were filled with all kinds of "Congratulations"—text messages, phone calls, emails, and Facebook messages, sometimes from people I didn't even know. The congratulatory messages came in quickly, too. The views on my blog skyrocketed from a couple of hundred to about 1500 in the course of two days. Hearing "Congratulations" from so many people made the whole experience seem real.

It had finally sunk in. Unlike the other graduating seniors in my college, I didn't have to worry about what I'd be doing next. I already knew. I was going to Disney World.

Chapter Five

*Our heritage and ideals, our code and standards—the things
we live by and teach our children—are preserved or dimin-
ished by how freely we exchange ideas and feelings.*

As a future Disney College Program participant, a few things in my
life have changed rather quickly. Random people I've conversed
with have gone from horrified (at my future history degree with
no post-graduation plans) to amazed that I will be pursuing a paid
internship next fall with one of the most well-respected companies
in the world. At the same time, others have looked down on the
program and wondered why on Earth I would do such a thing.

"So you're going to *Disney* College? Are you going to learn how to
be Mickey or something?"

*Yes, I am actually paying a tuition fee and going to school to learn how
to be Mickey.* That is *obviously* the next logical step after graduating
with a bachelor's degree. But in all seriousness, I have encountered
a lot of people who have no idea what the program is; and if they do,
it's usually wrong. The most common misconception is that people
think it is a college. Rather than viewing the program as an internship, they view it as transferring to a different college and completing
a degree in, well...Disney, I guess. I assume that the name "Disney
College Program" is what leads to this misconception, but it makes
sense that it is not called something with "internship" in the title
because that would probably lead to even more confusion—there are
already "Disney Professional Internships", and they different from the
DCP. This is how I have been explaining the DCP to anyone who asks:

> The Disney College Program is a paid internship. Participants live
> in company-sponsored housing, work a number of different roles
> at locations across Disney property, and may attend classes and
> networking events.

Giving this little speech usually clears up any confusion, but every
now and then I get, "Do you have a dining hall/meal plan there?"

"So when is your vacation/winter break/spring break?" And perhaps the most obnoxious of all, "Can you get me into the parks for free?"

This last question, somewhat ironically, is often brought up by people who I am not very close with…at all. Almost immediately after I mentioned my acceptance into the DCP on Facebook, I began receiving messages from people I haven't seen or spoken to in years. That girl who was in my biology class for the two weeks before she switched schools when I was fifteen years old? Apparently she is planning on visiting Walt Disney World in December and wanted to know if she would be able to bring herself and three friends into the parks for free with my discount. Maybe it's just me, but I think it is just a little bit rude to message someone you have not spoken to in at least four years for your own personal benefit. Since making it known that I have been accepted, similar situations have happened, and are continuing to happen. (If my close friends or my family asked about discounts, I would not mind, but I am talking about people who I haven't seen or heard from in years, who all of a sudden want to be my best friend.)

After expecting both too much and too little from the DCP Facebook groups, I've come up with a simple piece of advice: Use them to find your roommates, and then get out. At the time of my acceptance, I was in six DCP Facebook groups: one for my program season, arrival date, role, roommates, group of friends, and participants who were in the Submission stage of the application.

The Submission stage is how Disney refers to the status of those applicants who have not been offered a Web-Based Interview, but have not been NLIC'ed either. While I was never stuck in Submission, Chaz was, so I joined the group in order to support him. The other members of this group were clearly, and understandably, frustrated as a result of not receiving a Web-Based Interview. Because of this, I was extremely careful to not post about my acceptance in this group—I did not want to remind the other members that I was further ahead of them in the process. In addition to showing support for Chaz, I tried to be supportive of the other group members who were in the same situation.

One of my comments on the Submission Facebook page was captured in a screenshot by a member of the group and emailed to Disney. I received an email from Disney, with the screenshot attached and a recruiter's response to what I wrote. My comment was in response to another screenshot that someone else had posted in the group, referring to an email she had received from Disney telling her that applications were still being accepted for the program. I posted that one would think there would be a way for Disney to filter out those emails, so that students who have already applied but have not yet heard back would not have to be reminded that they were stalled in the process. The Disney recruiter who wrote to me explained how Disney determines which emails to send to which people. I was already aware of everything in the email, and I was not sure if the tone was meant to be informative or angry. Was my acceptance in jeopardy because I had innocently posted a comment on a Facebook page? The recruiter went on to explain that people who received reminder emails had opted in (and thus had asked for them), and that while I might follow the official DCP blog, where important information about the program is communicated, others might not.

The response was weird, because I hadn't meant to complain about Disney's automated emails; I was just trying to be supportive of the Facebook member who had posted the screenshot, since she was obviously disappointed when she received an email from Disney's recruiting department that was *not* an invitation to take the WBI. I was worried that I was in some kind of trouble with Disney. Receiving an email with a screenshot of something you said on Facebook from a future employer does not impart a warm and fuzzy. Luckily, nothing more came of it, and I'm still scratching my head over why Disney went to such trouble to send me an email in the first place—as well as why someone would go to even greater trouble to take a screenshot of my comment and report it to Disney!

Did a disgruntled member of the Submission group "report" me to Disney because he or she had deduced I'd been accepted into the program and had no business being among those who hadn't? I'll never know. But I left the group shortly after I got the email from Disney.

Holly and I finally found enough roommates to fill an apartment. The process of finding our other two roommates was in reality fairly quick, though it felt as if it took forever because of how many potential roommates came and went before we fixed on Paulina and Lexie.

Initially, Holly and I had planned on rooming with Kaitie, and finding at least one other person to fill an apartment. When Kaitie did not pass the Web-Based Interview, finding roommates was put on the back-burner. Not only were we saddened to hear that Kaitie would not be moving on, but her interview results gave us the much-needed reality check that looking for more roommates before we were *all* accepted was not the best idea.

Holly and I discussed simply getting a one bedroom apartment, but we decided that they looked really small (from the apartment tours we'd watched on YouTube) and would that we would prefer something bigger, with more roommates. Eventually, we made a post in the August 4 Arrival Facebook group (there's a Facebook group for virtually *everything* about the DCP), describing ourselves and stating that we were looking for two more roommates to fill a two bedroom apartment. We described ourselves as responsible and respectful, but still interested in going out and having a lot of fun during our program. Both Holly and I would graduate from college before the start of our programs, so without the pressure of taking classes, we wanted to experience everything that Orlando had to offer, and we wanted roommates who felt the same. We also were looking to fill a Non-Wellness apartment, preferably in Vista Way. Non-Wellness means that everyone living there is over 21 years old, and so we could have alcohol in the partment. (If Disney finds alcohol in a Wellness, or under 21, apartment, the people living there could be "termed"—Disney-speak for fired from the program.)

The next day I received a message on Facebook from Paulina, which included a link to an "About Me" video on YouTube for Holly and I to watch. Paulina was perfect for our apartment—she was outgoing, funny, polite, and could be serious at times, but also wanted to have fun in Florida. Paulina was in. One down, one to go.

Thankfully, Holly and I did not need to look for any more room-mates— Paulina suggested that her friend Lexie, who was also recently accepted into the DCP, live with us to fill the extra bedroom. Lexie's personality meshed with ours, and both she and Paulina fit the main requirement that Holly and I looked for in other roommates— that they have lived with roommates before, which we believe covers a lot of the typical roommate issues that can arise with people who have never lived away from home.

The DCP, and I would argue college in general, is interesting for my generation in that so many students find roommates online. Someone from an older generation may read this book and think that the process I went through to find roommates through Facebook was a little odd, but this method is quickly becoming the norm. For someone who doesn't use the internet for, well, pretty much everything, finding someone to live with for five months online may be terrifying. But I never would have wanted to be randomly assigned a roommate, and I know from my experience in college that whatever roommate survey the institution gives you (to find someone you're "compatible" with) does not necessarily work, either. I ended up switching roommates halfway through my freshman year of college, which resulted in me ultimately living with Theresa, a girl I "met" via the Saint Anselm Class of 2014 Facebook page before arriving on campus. Theoretically, it would have made a lot of sense to live with Theresa from the beginning, but I shied away from living with someone I met online.

Like it or not, and I don't particularly like it, meeting people online is the way of the future. Many college students get to know each other on Facebook groups before they move into their dorms, and the DCP is no different.

To make our in-person meeting in Orlando as comfortable as possible, my roommates and I added each other on every social media outlet out there—Twitter, Instagram, Snapchat, and all the rest. We've exchanged phone numbers so we can text on a regular basis. And most importantly, we've had Google Hangouts. Google Hangouts are basically webcam sessions that we can all take part in. I feel so much better knowing that I will be living with these girls after speaking with them "face-to-face". The whole situation is still strange, because it isn't really face-to-face, and no matter how safe finding roommates online seems, you are always taking a little bit of a risk. I'm pretty sure at this point we've all done what amounts to full background checks on each other, but it's just worth noting how much of a process it is to find and get to know your roommates online.

Chapter Six

*Times and conditions change so rapidly that we must
keep our aim constantly focused on the future.*

By April, my own application process had come to an end; for Chaz, however, it had never really begun. We had both submitted our applications on the same day—February 6, 2014—and while I was asked to complete a Web-Based Interview that same day, Chaz's application remained in the Submission phase, which means that it has undergone an initial review and is still being considered.

The Submission stage was a new concept to me. The first time I applied for the DCP, there was no such thing as a Submission stage—as far as I know, every applicant in 2011 was offered a WBI. As of 2014, some applicants will never receive a WBI, and without one they will not be able to move on with the application process. On the first day, when I completed my WBI and scheduled my phone interview, Chaz waited for an email from Disney that never came, we knew that we could be split up. In applying for the DCP with your significant other, there is always the chance that only one of you will get in, and we tried to think of this eventuality in the most realistic way possible, while still hoping that we would both be accepted.

March 31, 2014, Chaz's 25th birthday, came and went without an invitation to take the WBI. The last day that Disney could make a decision about the status of an application was April 18, and with this deadline approaching, we decided that it would not hurt to send the recruiting department an email. What Chaz sent was essentially a cover letter. It explained that he was still interested in the program, and would greatly appreciate the opportunity to be considered, as decisions were drawing to a close. The email went over his work experience and qualifications, and how he thought his participation in the program would benefit both himself and the company. His resume was attached. We knew his chances were slim, but with the acceptance deadline just two weeks away, we figured it couldn't hurt.

That evening Chaz received an automated response promising an update on his application in 3-5 business days. At that point, Chaz's application status was still out of our hands, and all we could do was wait some more. *A great birthday present would have been an invitation for the WBI.*

The following afternoon, on April 1, 2014, Chaz finally received an update from Disney College Program Recruiting:

> Dear Chaz,
>
> Thank you for taking the time to express your interest in the Disney College Program.
>
> We have reviewed your information. Unfortunately, at this time you are not being considered for this opportunity.
>
> If you are interested in applying in the future, please visit disneycollegeprogram.com. Please note you can only apply once per recruiting season (February to April and September to November).
>
> Thank you again for your interest in the Disney College Program.
>
> Best regards,
>
> Disney College Recruiting

And with that, Chaz was NLIC'ed (no longer in consideration) for the Disney College Program. At first, he took it better than I did—I was aggravated, because this made me think that they did not read the email he had sent the day before, and while the chances of it influencing Disney's decision were probably close to nil anyway, I was still hopeful. I should also point out that we noticed through the Facebook groups that other applicants began receiving rejection letters days before him, so I took it as a good sign that he remained in Submission for so long. When he logged in to check his Dashboard on April 1, his status had not yet changed. Generally, when Disney stops considering you for a position, your status changes from Submission to No Longer in Consideration. Chaz's status was still Submission, which also made his Dashboard different from other members of the Facebook group who were receiving rejection emails.

Chaz was beginning to feel discouraged, and he wondered if he should consider applying for the Spring 2015 program in September. After learning that the status on his Dashboard had not changed, I told him that he should call the recruiting department to see whether they had reviewed his email and resume. I've heard of very rare instances where applicants have been rejected and later accepted, due to some sort of mistake by the recruiters. While these instances are rare, I wondered if that was what had happened to Chaz, since his status did not change on his Dashboard. My optimistic personality took control here, as I was actually mildly convinced that they had sent him a rejection email by mistake and he was still being considered.

He did call the recruiting office, and midway through his conversation with them he saw on his Dashboard that his status had finally changed to No Longer in Consideration. He did ask about the email he had sent, but he received the standard response from the recruiter—that they would likely get around to responding to it in 3-5 business days. (They never did respond; I assume that the No Longer in Consideration email was their response.)

And with that, Chaz's application process for the Disney College Program Fall 2014 season had truly come to an end.

Chapter Seven

For every laugh there should be a tear.

Summer came and went, and my check-in date for the DCP arrived faster than I expected. On August 3, 2014, I left Massachusetts and boarded my flight to Orlando. Saying good-bye to my friends and family at home was not as difficult as you might imagine—probably because I had already lived away at school, and the DCP is only an internship, so I would be home again after I complete it. The most difficult good-bye I had to make was with Chaz, not so much because we're together, but because I still felt bad that I was accepted and he was not. Even though he was proud of me, it was difficult to leave and go off on this adventure that we had planned on doing together.

Holly picked me up from the Orlando airport that afternoon so that I wouldn't need to pay for a cab to the hotel where we were staying. You might think that meeting your roommate for the first time would be awkward, especially when she is picking you up from the airport and spending a night in your hotel room, but it really wasn't. I assume this was because Holly and I had talked so much before we arrived; it felt like we already knew each other.

Before checking into our hotel on International Drive, Holly and I drove to the Boardwalk Inn to check out the shops and relax. After a much-needed lunch at the ESPN Zone (which included a delicious BBQ chicken sandwich, I might add), we walked over to the entrance to World Showcase in Epcot. Looking back, I'm not exactly sure why we did so. All that we accomplished was to torture ourselves, as we could not enter the theme parks for free until we received our Walt Disney Company IDs later in the week. For about 30 seconds, we actually thought about purchasing a 1-day ticket for Epcot (at $94), but we quickly regained our common sense.

After what amounted to the saddest visit to Epcot ever, we hopped back in the car and drove to International Drive to check in to our hotel. It was close to a number of shops and restaurants, so we spent some time walking around this part of Orlando. It was fun to browse the shops on "I-Drive", especially because I have never been outside of Walt Disney World during all of my previous visits to Orlando. I never realized how many tourists stay on I-Drive and do all kinds of other touristy things (like museums, bars, restaurants, and shopping) rather than staying within one of the theme parks.

Holly and I went back to our hotel room at around 9:00 pm, in the belief that we should get to bed early to check in the next day. By the time we were back in our hotel room, we both had headaches and could not figure out why we felt so crappy. Then suddenly it dawned on us that all we had eaten that day was the sandwiches at the Boardwalk. This would become a theme for the first couple of days of the DCP—during the first week, I felt like I had so much to do that I hardly had time to eat. That night in the hotel, we ended up ordering tea and pizza from room service, and we eventually felt better and were able to fall asleep...for a couple of hours, anyway. We were both excited and couldn't wait to check in the next day, so getting enough sleep was not easy that night. The two of us woke up at about 3:00 am and tossed and turned until dawn.

We eventually got out of bed and began to get ready at about 7:00 am on August 4. We had to be at the Vista Way apartment complex for check-in at 9:00 am. Even though we arrived right around the appointed time, the line wasn't nearly as bad as I had expected.

When I had researched the program in previous years, most participants mentioned how long the line was at check-in, and how they needed to be there as early as 4:00 am to secure a spot in their first choice of housing. By the time of my program, Disney had changed their check-in policy. Rather than waiting outside of Vista Way, basically overnight, participants are now assigned a time when they can check in. This has all been made possible by DORMS, a program that Disney uses to record each CP's (short for "college program participant") housing and roommate preferences so that they can have a greater chance of getting their first choices without waiting in line. Filling out the DORMS paperwork is extremely easy. About a week before CPs leave to start their program, they now receive emails from Disney with links to paperwork they can complete and submit before their arrival. The first choice of housing for my roommates and I was Vista Way. Our next choices were any of the other apartment complexes which had two bedrooms for four CPs. (Some of the bedrooms in Disney housing are now triple occupancy, and we wanted to avoid that as much as we possibly could.)

Though our spot in line theoretically did not matter, like it would have before DORMS was introduced, Holly and I managed to be pretty close to the front. The check-in process begins at the Vista Way Welcome Center, and we only needed to wait in line for about a half an hour before we were helped. While in line, we were given our temporary name tags (just little labels with our names written on them) and our program guides. The program guide contains everything you would ever need to know about your program. There are maps of all of the housing complexes, information on the Disney Look, tips for passing inspections, and general advice and information about nearly anything that could come up during the program.

Once inside the welcome center, we were given stickers to place in the back of our program guides that had our names and some other basic information such as our Perner numbers. The Perner number is Disney's version of a company ID. You use it for a variety of things, such as clocking in and out of work, getting work assignments, and receiving Cast Member discounts.

At the next turn in the queue inside the welcome center, Holly and I were split up. This is where we found out our specific work locations… well, they were somewhat specific, anyway. Holly went up to the counter before me and learned that she was placed in Attractions for Adventureland/Liberty Square in the Magic Kingdom. Her first choice of a work location was Jungle Cruise, so it was now highly likely that this was where she would be placed, though she would not find out for sure until she began training.

When it was my turn to go to the next counter, I was given a sticker for the last page of my program guide which contained good news and bad news. The good news was that I was placed in Animal Kingdom. After learning that I had been accepted for Merchandise, Animal Kingdom was my first choice for where I would want to work. I love the park, and I knew that I would love the hours if I were to work there. Animal Kingdom closes earlier than the other parks, so by working there I would not have the typical late nights that most CPs are forced to work. The bad news was that I had been placed in DinoLand U.S.A.—my least favorite area in all of Walt Disney World. Almost nothing about Merchandise in DinoLand appealed to me. I knew the costume would be horrendous, and I just didn't get the atmosphere of Chester and Hester's Dino-Rama when I visited the area as a guest. All Disney costumes are unflattering, but I was looking forward to wearing something fun, and while the DinoLand costume is definitely meant to be "fun", it is also horribly tacky. While I was not excited about my work location, I did not let it get to me during check-in. I was still ecstatic to be here, and I looked at it as a compromise: I wanted to be placed in Animal Kingdom, and that's where I was placed, albeit in the worst part of the park.

As I moved into the next queue, Holly caught my attention from the end of the next counter, where she yelled to me that she was placed in Vista Way, our first choice. She told me her apartment number as she moved through the line so that I would know immediately if we had been placed in the same apartment. At the next counter, I learned that we were indeed in the same apartment: #510 in Vista Way. We still had not seen our other prospective roommates, though we knew from texting them that they were much farther back in the line outside the welcome center. I texted both of them to let them know that Holly and I were both in 510, so our hopes were high that the four of us would be together, as planned.

After receiving my apartment number, I got into yet another line where I was given the key. The key was taped onto the back page of my program guide, along with the other sticker containing my unfortunate work location. Next up for check-in, I needed to get my photo taken for my housing ID. As a CP, your housing ID is extremely important. You need it to get on the CP bus, and if I walk or drive (even as a passenger in someone else's car) into the apartment complex, I need my ID to be let in.

Upon receiving my ID, which was printed immediately after my photo was taken, I was ushered outside the center where I learned the first couple of days of my training schedule. This is where I was completely split up from Holly, as her schedule had her taking the 10:30 am bus to Casting, and mine had me taking the 11:30 am bus. Holly finished up with the welcome center portion of check-in and headed for the bus, while I was brought to a round table outside the center with about five other CPs and a program coordinator who went over some basic things about our schedule. The coordinator pointed out that we would need to go to the Casting building at our scheduled time, and there we would fill out some paperwork, be fingerprinted for our background checks, and learn the rest of our training schedules. She explained that we needed to wear business attire for our Traditions class, and that we should be at the bus stop on time. I'm not quite sure what would happen if you are late to your Traditions class, but by the sounds of it I didn't want to risk it and find out. If you're a future CP, and all of this sounds tedious and overwhelming to you, don't worry—everything I was told during check-in was either on the paperwork I was given or in the program guide, so as long as you know how to read, you'll be okay. On a similar note, I wish Disney would have acknowledged that I do indeed know how to read so that the check-in process could have been cut a bit shorter.

Once the coordinator finished reiterating what was clearly written on the handout in front of me, I moved on to the next table where another person confirmed that my weekly pay would be direct deposited into my bank account. CPs have the option to use either direct deposit or a payroll card (basically a prepaid debit card), though I've found that most CPs, myself included, prefer direct deposit.

I was on my way to the bus stop for Casting when I met Lexie, one of my other roommates. She told me that she was in the same apartment as Holly and myself, and that she was still waiting for Paulina, the last of our roommates (we hoped!) to find out where she was placed. Lexie's role was Attractions, in Epcot's Future World East. She was scheduled to take the same bus to Casting as me, so we were able to go through the Casting process together. Before the bus came, a couple of DCP coordinators gave us tote bags with some granola bars, first aid kits, and laundry detergent inside. A representative from the education portion of the DCP also came by and gave us handouts about classes and mentioned that we can still enroll in some of the course offerings if we chose. I wanted to take Disney Heritage, but I had been waitlisted so I opted for Exploring Marketing instead. Because I was waitlisted for my first choice already, it kind of annoyed me that someone told me "there's still time to enroll!" but she was just doing her job. Enrolling for Disney's classes was the same as enrolling for classes in college. It was done online, and it was likely that you would be waitlisted for the ones you wanted most.

The bus ride to Casting was surprisingly eventful. A DCP coordinator was on the bus and told us a number of Disney jokes and asked us Disney trivia questions to keep us entertained. Lexie answered one of the questions correctly and was given a DCP pin. The coordinator also did a great job of keeping everyone's energy up after we'd been standing in line after line during check-in. As we passed under the "Welcome to Walt Disney World" gate for the first time, the coordinator had the entire bus count down and cheer. This extra excitement made us even more anxious to get the Casting process over with so we could finally get settled in our apartments, get our training over with, and step foot for the first time as Cast Members in the parks.

When we arrived at the Casting building, I was stunned by its beauty. I had expected an ordinary office building, but this was Disney after all, and I shouldn't have expected anything less. The building's façade was somewhat whimsical, with light pink paint and teal-colored fixtures, but the decorative highlight of the building's exterior was the door knobs at the entrance—they were exact replicas of the door knobs from *Alice in Wonderland*. Once inside, we waited in another line, this time in the front lobby of the building, where we were greeted by gold statues of Disney characters. As the line moved, we were taken in groups down the first hallway, which featured professional photos of Disney Cast Members who were clearly enjoying themselves at work. As I passed by the photos, I heard one of the Cast Members who worked in the building congratulate us and mention that those photos will be us soon. Our time here was mostly another series of lines with more forms to fill out, reading more paperwork, and being reminded of things that I had already confirmed I understood when I filled out the initial application. We were also fingerprinted, and we had meetings with some other coordinators who gave us further details about our training schedules.

The meeting with my coordinator consisted of him giving me a training schedule and circling and highlighting the important parts, like the places where I had to be and the times when I had to be there. My training schedule included DAKlimations, the introduction class for Animal Kingdom Cast Members; Merchantainment for Merchandise Cast Members; Welcome to Operations, which most Disney Cast Members need to complete; and Traditions, which anyone who works for Disney must take.

And with that, I was done with Casting. The whole process only took about two hours, though I've heard it can take much longer depending on the length of the lines and how quickly you're moved along. Someday I would love to go back to the Casting building just to look at all of the decorations and artwork in there—I really did not expect the building to be anything special, and it would be interesting to spend some time there without the pressure of paperwork and lines.

Instead of taking the bus from Casting back to Vista, Lexie's parents came to pick us up. It was so much more convenient to have a ride than to wait for the bus; we were back in Vista while everyone else was still at Casting, waiting for one of the notoriously slow Transtar buses to arrive. By 2 pm we were opening the door to our apartment and there was Holly already inside. This was the first time the three of us had all been in the same room together. Paulina was probably still at the Casting building, and we did not yet know if she had been placed in our apartment. We spent some time looking around the apartment, and examining how it was furnished and whether everything worked (as far as we could tell, it did), when suddenly there was a knock on the door. Holly answered, with Lexie and I not far behind, and we saw Paulina. We all screamed in delight as soon as we saw that it was her, and I think we all breathed a collective sigh of relief now that we were all together in the shared apartment we wanted, and in the apartment complex we wanted, too.

Within the next couple of hours, Lexie's parents left and we got down to the task of unpacking and organizing the apartment. The first thing we noticed was that our apartment seriously needed to be cleaned. Because it had been recently renovated, it appeared that some of the dirtiness was the result of the construction crews not cleaning up after themselves. The sink fixtures looked like they had just been put in, and the floor was in desperate need of a mop. The blinds and window sills in our living room were also sort of dirty. I wasn't sure whether that was the fault of the previous occupants or the construction crew, but either way the housing maintenance department should have had all the mess cleaned up before we moved in. The worst part of it was the kitchen. The dishes and silverware did not look like they had been cleaned very well, if at all, by the last occupants, and it was unclear if the dishwasher was working properly. Without wasting too much time worrying about the kitchen, we loaded the dishwasher and packed into Paulina's car to go to Wal-Mart.

This trip to Wal-Mart was the most hectic and unpleasant shopping experience I think I've ever had. For starters, the Wal-Mart in Orlando near CP housing is huge and overwhelming. In addition to the usual Orlando tourist junk, the entire front portion of the store was essentially a cheapened Disney store. About half of the store was devoted to groceries and the other half (not including the bargain Disney stuff) was typical Wal-Mart stock. This store had to be at least double the size of the closest Wal-Mart (with grocery section) to me at home in Massachusetts. And the crowds! It seemed that every other CP who had checked in that day had the same idea as us, to take a trip to the local Wal-Mart and stock up on supplies, because the aisles were congested with college students like ourselves, and we often overheard snippets of conversation about Disney and "the program". In hindsight, we should have spent the day unpacking and then come to Wal-Mart tomorrow, but now that we were here, we decided to just get it over with now, crowds or not.

In addition to all of the cleaning supplies that our apartment desperately needed, we also bought some food staples. Since I had brought with me only what I could cram into a suitcase, I needed to buy even more. We each bought a couple of items that we would all be using in the apartment, such as a mop and dishwasher soap, and we decided that all of our food would be purchased individually. I was fine with this arrangement, though I didn't buy much this trip, just eggs, milk, bread, peanut butter, jelly, and some fruit. I've learned that Wal-Mart, at least the Orlando location, is not the place to go for produce. A lot of the produce I saw looked like it had been out on the shelves for way too long, and being the germaphobe that I am, I was grossed out so much by the store itself that it was difficult for me to want to purchase any kind of food from there.

By the time we finished shopping, it was about 7 pm, and we had two shopping carts loaded with all kinds of food and household items. As soon as we went outside, it started to rain, which quickly turned into heavy downpours. And with that, we had experienced our first bout of Florida weather. We tried to pack everything into the car as quickly as possible, but we didn't have much luck. With the two shopping carts worth of stuff, and the four of us also in the car, making everything fit was a tight squeeze, and it took some rearranging. Desperate to get home (to the kitchen we could not cook in because we hadn't cleaned it yet), we stopped for takeout—this would be one of the few times I had takeout during my program. Without a car it was nearly impossible to get, unless I had it delivered, but that would have meant an additional fee and a tip, and I'd still have to walk to the security checkpoint of my complex to pick up my "delivery".

Even though we were all exhausted, we started to clean the apartment that night, but soon gave it up and began to unpack, instead. Soon, however, the issue of who would be in each of the two bedrooms arose. The bedrooms in our apartment were very similar, but there were a couple of slight differences. One bedroom (the one I saw as less desirable) was located near the front door. To me, this meant that every time someone went in or out of the apartment, it would be relatively loud from inside that bedroom. The shape of the bedroom was also a little odd, in that there was no way to rearrange the furniture. Everything in this bedroom would need to stay the way it was, because there was nowhere else for it to go. The other downside was the shower. The shower in the bathroom portion of the first bedroom contained a flat floor, which to me means that there is nowhere to put your leg up while shaving. The bathroom in the other bedroom had a tub, so you could put your leg up on the edge of the tub and shave that way—just personal preference, I guess. The layout of the other bedroom also allowed for the rearranging of the furniture, and I felt that even a tiny bit of customization would make the place seem more like home.

After we finished bringing the groceries inside, Holly and I were relaxing for a moment when Lexie came up to us.

"Do you mind if Paulina and I take this bedroom?" she said, motioning toward what I considered to be the better of the two options.

I looked over at Holly, who also appeared to prefer that bedroom, and for a moment we were both silent.

"If you guys also want it, we could flip a coin or something." Lexie offered.

Holly and I ended up telling her that it was fine, that she and Paulina could have that room. Holly did mention later that it would have been nice to not be right next to the door, but we both figured that the differences in the bedrooms were not that big of a deal, and Lexie had asked nicely, so it would just be easier all around to let them have it.

Once the bedroom situation was settled, Holly and I chose our beds and began unpacking. We only unpacked the necessities that night, as everyone was exhausted and just wanted to go to sleep. I unpacked some pajamas, made my bed up with the mattress cover, new sheets, pillows, and comforter, and finally went to sleep. It was my first night on Disney property.

Chapter Eight

*Give the public everything you can give them. Keep the
place as clean as you can keep it. Keep it friendly.*

The next morning we all attended a mandatory housing meeting.
Holly and I were scheduled for the same meeting, at 11:30 am, while
Lexie and Paulina's meetings were either later in the day or the next
day after Traditions. Holly drove us to the meeting, which was held
in the Commons clubroom. The Commons is another one of the
DCP housing complexes. It used to be limited to only international
students, but in 2013 it was opened up to everyone. The other complexes—the Commons, Patterson Court, and Chatham Square—are
all very close to each other, whereas Vista Way is a bit more isolated.
I still preferred Vista, especially because of the convenience in being
able to walk to a nearby Walgreens since I did not bring a car.

The DCP staff at the housing meeting covered all of the basics that
you would expect to be discussed in any type of housing meeting at
college. Not surprisingly, since it's put on by Disney, this meeting
was much more entertaining than a college meeting, as there were
light effects and music. The focus was to let us know about all the
many things we were not allowed to do in CP housing.

The staff running the meeting gave us a quick overview of how
security would work for getting in and out of our housing complexes.
If I take the Transtar bus from anywhere to my complex, I need to
show my housing ID to get on the bus. If I walk outside of my complex
(to Walgreens, for instance), I have to stop at security and show my
housing ID to be let back in. If someone drives me to my apartment,
everyone in the car must show a housing ID (or be signed in as a
guest if they do not live in housing, which requires them to fill out a
form and leave a photocopy of their own photo ID). And no overnight
visitors from other complexes, ever.

The next topic of discussion was kind of a buzzkill. One of the managers for the college program told us about all the many different horrible

things that can happen to you while living in Florida. While he was just trying to be realistic and protect us, it put a damper on the mood of the meeting. He told us about how the party buses that stop outside the complexes are not affiliated with Disney, and how bad things can happen to you on a party bus. The bus owners charge a small fee to bring you to bars and clubs in Orlando, which generally works out to be cheaper than driving yourself and paying covers. Because the buses are not affiliated with Disney, we don't really know who else could be on them, so the DCP manager was—in so many words telling us that we could be raped, drugged, or killed, and that it wouldn't be Disney's fault. This segment also included a brief discussion of something I'd consider to be common sense: "Don't leave your drink unattended at the bar." The other issue he brought up with the party buses was underage drinking. If any CPs are in the presence of someone underage who is drinking and they are caught, all of those CPs will be termed from the program. So if there is a party bus with 20 people on it, and one of those people is 19 and drinking, and Disney somehow finds out about it, every CP on the bus is termed. On the plus side, party buses prevent people from drinking and driving, so at least there's that.

In addition to the party buses, the manager told us that Florida outside of Disney is a bad place. The next depressing information he gave us centered around the terrible drivers that are always in Orlando due to it being such a large tourist destination and all-around bad place to be. He told us about an ICP (International College Program participant) who was killed in 2012 while crossing the street in Orlando, and so we should always walk in groups, use crosswalks, look both ways, and avoid crossing busy streets in general, especially at night. This part of the housing meeting drained everyone emotionally, as there was absolutely nothing positive about learning of an ICP student who was killed by a careless driver while working for Disney.

Now that everyone was in a proper state of gloom, it was time to move on to the topic of things that are prohibited from CP housing. The leaders in charge of this part of the meeting awkwardly tried to be entertaining in an effort to lighten the mood—by using props. These props were items that had belonged to CPs who Disney termed from the program because they had been caught with these very items in their possession. The first item they showed us was a candle—no open flames/candles allowed in CP housing. Next they showed us a fish bowl, to represent how we were not allowed to have pets, even fish.

A shot glass was up next, though these were only prohibited from Wellness apartments (meaning that the people in that apartment were under 21, though some might also be over 21, if they had requested a Wellness apartment and agreed to abide by its rules). A CP raised his hand and asked if shot glasses were allowed in Wellness apartments if they were being used as a toothpick holder, since that's what Disney markets them as in their gift shops—the answer was no, any alcohol paraphernalia is prohibited from Wellness apartments. Next up was a toy gun. Any weapons, or things that might be mistaken for weapons, are not allowed in CP housing. On the weapons front, they also showed us a light saber, which was not allowed as well...even though it is sold at Tattooine Traders, the gift shop at the end of the Star Tours ride, and is clearly not your typical weapon. Lastly, they showed us the biggest bong I have ever seen, and a hookah, both clearly not allowed in CP housing, as they are considered drug paraphernalia.

Once we were shown all of the items that we cannot have in housing, we were shown a video of the events that the housing committee puts on during the program: welcome events, pool parties, bingo, a formal, and graduation, among others.

When the housing meeting was over, Holly and I decided to walk to the outlets located across the street from the Commons. We didn't buy much, but it at least gave us something to do since we could not get into the parks for free until after our Traditions class. Shopping, or at least window shopping, was the theme of the first couple of days of the DCP, because there was pretty much nothing else to do unless we wanted to go to another theme park, which no one wanted to pay for so soon after blowing a big chunk of cash at Wal-Mart.

Later that day, I went to Downtown Disney with Lexie. We ate at Earl of Sandwich for the first time (which was delicious) and looked around World of Disney. I did buy a couple of things at World of Disney, but they were things I actually needed for my apartment, like a coffee mug (with Elsa on it) and a Mickey spatula.

The rest of the day was uneventful—just more cleaning up the apartment and unpacking and much-needed sleep, since I was still exhausted from moving in. Thankfully, my roommates and I were all off the next evening, so we were able to go out for our first roommate dinner. We went to Kona Café, at the Polynesian, my favorite restaurant in Disney World. Again, it was a tease to see the Magic Kingdom and not be able to go, but we only needed to wait one more day.

Warning: spoilers ahead. If you want to be surprised by Traditions, do not read the rest of this chapter.

The next day I was scheduled for the morning Traditions class, where I would receive my company ID and finally be able to go to the parks! Traditions is a class that every Disney Cast Member must take before they can begin training with the company. I had heard good things about this class after talking to former CPs, so I was excited. I was not, however, excited about getting up early enough to make the 6:00 am bus. For whatever reason, we were encouraged to take the bus rather than drive to Traditions (it didn't make a difference to me; since I had no car, I would have needed to take the bus anyway). There was also an afternoon class, but I'm happy I was placed in the morning class because I was able to go to one of the parks later that day. The afternoon class would not have left much time for that.

For all training at Disney that you are not in costume for, you must be in business attire. Some of the outfits people wore to Traditions that they apparently believed passed as business attire was insane. *If you don't know what business attire looks like, you need to rethink undertaking a highly competitive internship with a Fortune 500 company, because frankly you will look like an idiot.* I, like most CPs, wore business attire to all of my Disney classes, which was extremely uncomfortable in Florida heat and humidity since I was so used to the weather up north. Do not complain to me that you're hot while walking around the parks until you've done it in black dress pants, a blouse, and a black blazer during the hottest month of the year.

Traditions was held at Disney University, a classroom facility located behind the Magic Kingdom. Upon our arrival, we lined up outside the building and were divided into different groups. Each group was assigned a classroom, and we followed our leaders inside the building to the room where we'd be spending most of the day. Disney University, much like the Casting building, had a lot to look at inside. The walls were lined with Disney artwork, as well as information about some of the Disney Legends and other random tidbits about the company's history. Also located inside Disney University is one of two Company D locations. The other Company D is located in Epcot's Cast Services building. Company D sells cast member exclusive merchandise and discounted park and event tickets. In addition, there is also a cast cafeteria inside Disney University.

My roommate Paulina and I were placed in the same classroom for Traditions, so we got seats together at one of the tables near the front of the room with four other girls who coincidentally would all be working Merchandise in Animal Kingdom, just like me. The other Merchandise girls were not in DinoLand, though—they were on Discovery Island, the location I was really going for when I decided I'd like to be placed in Animal Kingdom. Before class began, we needed to sign our names on a roster so that the instructors would know we were present. As we were seated at our tables, waiting for class to begin, we looked at the television screen toward the front of the class to see that our names were flashing across it on monogramed Mickey ears. It is the little touches like this that make training for Disney such a special experience. We also noticed a red gift box, complete with a ribbon tied in a bow, on our tables. Of course, everyone wanted to know what was inside the box, but we were told by our instructors that we needed to wait to open them.

Before any class at Disney University can start, you are forced to watch a safety video about how to evacuate the building. It's about 5 minutes long, but it is literally the most boring video you would ever watch. Every time I went to a new class during my program and the instructor went to play the safety video, the entire class groaned.

As class got started, our instructors began to tell us about themselves. They had both started working for Disney through the Disney College Program. They had performed a number of roles in the company, and from what I understood at the time (with my then-limited knowledge of how upward mobility with Disney worked) they currently had somewhat decent but not necessarily higher-up jobs with the company. They did mention that it was an honor for them to be chosen to teach Traditions, and how competitive the process is to become a Traditions instructor. Cast Members who are selected to teach Traditions classes are only able to do so for one calendar year.

Much of Traditions was focused around the experiences of other Cast Members as they explained why they enjoy working for Disney and fulfilling their roles to the best of their ability. This is when it became extremely clear that this is not the kind of job you take for the money. At one point during Traditions, one of our instructors read aloud a letter that a guest had written to Guest Relations about an experience she had had with a Disney Cast Member during her vacation. The woman who wrote the letter explained that she had a very young, very ill daughter, who was paralyzed from the waist down. Her daughter was in a wheelchair, unable to transfer out of it to experience many of the attractions in Walt Disney World, but simply being there and experiencing the parades and shows was really what she wanted out of her vacation, so it didn't matter too much. The mother mentioned how her family visited Animal Kingdom, where they enjoyed watching one of their favorite Disney shows, Festival of the Lion King. In the beginning of the show, some of the performers choose children from the audience to parade around the stage with the rest of the cast. One of the Cast Members performing in the show chose the wheelchair-bound daughter of the guest who wrote the letter. While the young girl was not able to dance around the stage herself, the Cast Member pushed her wheelchair through the line with the other children, while the girl smiled and clapped and enjoyed being a part of one of her favorite shows. This experience was recounted in the letter that the girl's mother had written, along with some extra commentary. The mother mentioned that it was impossible for her family to feel "normal" during their day-to-day lives, and that each and every day, her daughter was inevitably going to feel different from other children. She wrote that the experience the Cast Member had made for her daughter at the Lion King show made her for once feel "normal", as she was able to have an identical experience to children who were not bound to a wheelchair. She went on to express her gratitude and appreciation for everything that Disney Cast Members do to go above and beyond to make each guest's visit as special as it can possibly be.

Next, we were shown actual video footage of the Cast Member inviting the girl up on stage and dancing along with her wheelchair during the parade portion of the show. Following the video was a response from that Cast Member, as he read the letter that was sent in about him to Guest Relations. He responded that he did not want the girl to feel different from the other kids, and to him she was no different. She was just another girl who enjoyed the show, and he wanted her to feel as welcome as everyone else. He was blown away by the letter, and repeatedly mentioned how he loved working for the company, because there is no other workplace that would allow you to create those kind of magical experiences during any given shift.

As everyone in the classroom collectively wiped the tears from their eyes, the instructors began to play some more informational, yet also touching videos. These videos included footage of Bob Iger, the CEO of the Walt Disney Company, and a variety of other Cast Members welcoming us to the team. The instructors also shared some personal experiences and magical moments that they had taken part in during their time with the company, before finally allowing us to open the box in front of us. The box contained a pair of black Mickey ears for each person at the table. As the instructors explained how special our first pair of ears as Cast Members was, everyone in the room began to tear up again. They also asked how many of the new Cast Members in the room had never had ears before and if this was their first pair. The new Cast Members who were holding their first pairs of ears were ecstatic, and it was a great experience to be able to share in this "first" with them.

After receiving our ears, we were sent on break. Everyone rushed to the cafeteria. The line for food was crazy, because so many new CPs had gotten there before me. I did not want to spend my entire break in line, so instead I went to Company D and looked around inside. Of course, I couldn't leave the store empty-handed, and I returned to the cafeteria with a Disney College Program exclusive pin and a Cast Member exclusive magnet. My lunch might have only been a Twix bar from the vending machine, but I consider my mini-shopping spree to be worth the sacrifice. When I returned to the cafeteria, I sat down at a table with some more Animal Kingdom merchandise CPs—none of whom, of course, had been placed in DinoLand. Perhaps I was just bitter because I strongly disliked DinoLand, but I was beginning to feel left out since I had not met anyone else who'd be working in my area. Every time I met a new CP who worked in Merchandise, it seemed like the conversation went as follows:

"I'm in Merchandise in Animal Kingdom, too!"

"No way! Where are you working?"

"I'm in DinoLand!"

"Oh, I'm in Main Entrance/Africa/Discovery Island/Asia."

You and everyone else in this Traditions class...

While everyone I met that day in the cafeteria was extremely nice, I was slightly annoyed that of an entire table of Animal Kingdom Merchandise CPs, I was the only DinoLand Cast Member. I stayed friends with some of the CPs I met that day throughout my program, and while it was nice getting to see them on the bus every now and then, it would have been nicer if I were able to work with them and easily rearrange shifts. As I came to learn later when I started working, DinoLand had significantly less CPs than other Merchandise locations, which made it more difficult to get to know CPs from my area outside of work.

When we returned to the classroom following our lunch, our instructors told us that we could pick up our company IDs on the table in the back of the room. We were so excited to finally have our blue IDs, because this meant that we could officially go to the parks for free! Before class resumed, our instructors gave us some information about our new IDs: we could only use them to get into the parks for free for about two weeks. After that period, we should receive our Main Gate passes in the mail, which we would then use for entry into the parks. Once we have our Main Gates, our blue IDs cannot even be used for backup. (Paulina once forgot her Main Gate in our apartment, and she was denied entry into Epcot. She needed to go all the way back to the apartment to get her Main Gate, even though it was clear that she worked for the company.) Our IDs also do not have a picture on them. I'm still not exactly sure why not. I would assume that there is no picture on ours because we're CPs, but I don't know what difference that makes. Almost anytime I use my ID for something I need to take out my license as well to show a photo, so having a photo on my company ID would be much more convenient. Another important fact about a Disney company ID is that it is used for a number of things, and you would be completely lost if you were to lose it. For instance, I need my ID to get to my work location. If I go backstage at Animal Kingdom (or anywhere for that matter), there is a "zoom gate", or revolving door, that does not revolve until I scan my ID. I also need my ID to receive merchandise and dining discounts, purchase discounted tickets, enroll in Disney classes, use the learning centers at my work locations or apartment, and set up access to the HUB (Disney's internal website for Cast Members).

After receiving our IDs, the instructors told us that there was a special guest at the door, and we could let him come in for a little bit during class. When they opened the door, Mickey was there, with another gift box in his hand. The room was buzzing about what was in the box, though we all knew deep down what it was—our nametags. One by one, we were called to the front of the class to receive our nametags and say hi to Mickey. During this ceremony, our instructors told us how much of an honor it was that we had been accepted into the Disney College Program and that we were about to embark on an amazing journey. As Mickey greeted everyone and handed out nametags, the eyes of the new CPs in the room began to well up with tears again. But there was still one more bit of excitement left for our Traditions class that day.

As Mickey handed out the last name tag and waved good-bye, our instructors told us that we'd be leaving the classroom for a backstage tour of the Magic Kingdom, which included a peek into the Utilidors. (The Utilidors are the series of rooms and hallways that make up the "first floor" of the Magic Kingdom, out of sight and off-limits to guests. The park itself is on the "second floor".) To embark on our secret backstage tour of the Magic Kingdom, we needed to go incognito. We were told to remove our nametags, which we had so anxiously put on, and we donned headsets so that we could hear our instructor without him yelling across the park. The classroom was split into two groups for the tour, most likely to make us less conspicuous to regular guests. During our trip to the park, we were told to look for examples of the Four Keys—Safety, Show, Courtesy, Efficiency—in action. (The Four Keys set the standard for everything that Disney Cast Members do. They are at the foundation of each and every training session and daily meeting, and I'll be discussing them in more detail later on.)

While my group began heading toward the park, our instructor asked if any of us had never been to Disney World before. A couple of CPs in my group admitted that this backstage tour would indeed be their first visit to a Disney park. Upon hearing this, our instructor decided to bring us into the park through a backstage entrance that opens into one of the alcoves off Main Street, U.S.A., so that the first time the "guests" in our group could see Main Street and Cinderella Castle before going backstage. Our instructor created an emotional journey for those first visit CPs, as well as the rest of us, as he asked if we were ready before opening the gate to the park. When the gate opened, the first timers eyes lit up as they looked all around at the buildings and took in the music and the sights of the glass and crystal arts shop across the street. A couple of guests noticed our slightly large group pop out from backstage, but in that moment no one could have been bothered to care what they thought. The first timers were enthralled by their first few seconds in the Magic Kingdom, and the rest of us were in shock that we would actually be working there.

As we turned up Main Street toward the castle, a couple of the newbies began to tear up again, causing a chain reaction with nearly everyone in the group. By the time we reached the pathway between Fantasyland and Tomorrowland, the entire group was holding back tears and (very poorly) attempting to focus on the task at hand— finding examples of the Four Keys.

Our destination was Storybook Circus, where we were able to freely wander about. Unfortunately for our instructor, I don't think anyone was looking for Four Keys examples; we were just enjoying our time walking around the park. *Did he really think I'd be watching for how many Cast Members picked up trash when I could be browsing the gift shops or watching a show?*

After spending some time in Storybook Circus, we went backstage and took the Utilidors to exit the park. Inside the Utilidors we saw the Mousketeria, the central Cast Member cafeteria for the Magic Kingdom, as well as lockers and a hair salon. The Utilidors were hectic and had color-coded signs for the different themed lands of the park to direct Cast Members to where they needed to go. While working in the Magic Kingdom would be really cool, I imagine navigating the Utilidors must take some getting used to. Even though I know my way around the park extremely well, I can't say I know my way around down here. Going through the Utilidors the first time as a CP is an experience in itself.

When we returned to the classroom, our instructors spoke a little more about some things we needed to know about working for the company. One aspect of Disney life he mentioned was character integrity. Character integrity is the "fact" that there is only one of each character, and that each character is real. Character integrity, to me, is a very interesting concept, and it comes with its own set of rules and regulations. For instance, if you are a Cast Member who works as the face character for Cinderella, you would not tell your family and friends, "I am Cinderella," rather you would say, "I'm friends with Cinderella." This wording emphasizes that you have connections with the princess, but of course you can't actually be Cinderella, because there is only one Cinderella, and you are not her. Character integrity also dictates that multiples of the same characters are not out in the same park at the same time, because as we know, there is only one of each. For instance, during Mickey's Not So Scary

Halloween Party, Jack Sparrow is not out for meet and greets during the parade, because he is in the parade, and there is only one Jack Sparrow, so he cannot possibly be in two places at once.

To further demonstrate the importance of character integrity, our instructors put on a little skit for us, where one of them was a Cast Member and one was a guest:

> Guest: I was wondering if there was anywhere else that we could meet Elsa and Anna? The line to meet them at Princess Fairytale Hall is 90 minutes, and we couldn't get Fastpasses.

> Cast Member: Unfortunately, the only place where the queen and princess are meeting with guests right now is Princess Fairytale Hall, so the stand-by line is going to be the best option to meet them. However, Anna and Elsa will be leaving the hall at 3:00 to greet guests in our parade, so you will definitely be able to see them then.

> Guest: So I either have to wait 90 minutes or see them from a distance in the parade. Why can't you just have another Anna and Elsa on Main Street or something?

> Cast Member: Well, there is only one Anna and one Elsa, and though Elsa's powers are pretty magical, I don't think they're magical enough to allow them to be in two places at once.

We also discussed the importance of show and courtesy while working for Disney. As part of show, our instructor asked us who was responsible for keeping the parks clean. A couple of CPs answered with "Custodial Cast Members", while the rest answered, "everyone", which was the correct answer. Our instructor then made the bold statement that we were all Custodial Cast Members. It is part of any Cast Member's job to pick up trash and clean when they see something messy. Of course, there are certain scenarios that require actual Custodial Cast Members to clean up because they have the proper chemicals that most other Cast Members do not have, but I'll get to that later on.

This is also when we were taught the "Disney Scoop". The Disney Scoop is the method of quickly and efficiently picking up trash from the ground, and it is something that all Disney Cast Members are expected to do. To perform the Disney Scoop, you simply reach down and scoop up the trash while still walking and deposit it into the nearest trash barrel, which should only be about 20 feet away. (Disney executives did research into how far people would walk before littering so that they knew where to place trash cans. Unfortunately, guests still litter occasionally, but it was an interesting idea.)

In discussing courtesy, we were taught to be fully engaged in each guest situation regardless of what was happening to us personally. This idea is pretty common sense for anyone who works in customer service; however, bad service would seem worse in Disney because guests' expectations are higher than they would be anywhere else. One example is giving directions. Telling a guest to take a right and then follow the signs to wherever they needed to go is not helpful. If the signs were sufficient, they wouldn't be asking for directions. Instead, you would tell the guests to take a right, and then give them a landmark that should be there, and then further directions, all while using the "Disney Point". The Disney Point is how Cast Members direct guests while pointing with either two fingers or with just their hand (fingers together). The main reason for pointing in this manner is that Walt Disney World is the most visited tourist attraction in the entire world, and in some cultures pointing with one finger is incredibly rude. Some say another reason is because Walt Disney always pointed with two fingers. Walt, however, was not doing this to be politically correct; he was doing it because he often had a cigarette positioned between his fingers while he was pointing.

Another way we learned to maintain show and courtesy for our guests was to wear our costumes properly and in keeping with the theme of the park while we were off the clock (depending on where we worked). For the Magic Kingdom this did not matter so much, because Cast Members would never be onstage while off the clock. But for Animal Kingdom, where I would be working, it mattered a great deal, because Cast Members who work in that park enter and exit through the regular entrance with guests. This meant that I should have my costume on properly while going to and from work, even though I was not clocked in. I should also not have headphones on, or anything else that would distract me from the environment. It also meant that I should continue to be courteous to guests, even though I would not be getting paid for it. If a guest asks a Cast Member a question while he or she is off the clock, it is expected that the guest would receive the same response as if the Cast Member was working.

After another "Welcome to the Team" video, our instructors closed the class by telling us how excited they were to have us as part of the company, and that our journey was just beginning...and that we could finally go to the parks for free!

We left Disney University and headed for the bus stop as fast as our dress shoes and business attire would allow.

Chapter Nine

Laughter is America's most important export.

Immediately following Traditions, Holly, Paulina, Lexie, and I rushed back to our apartment to change out of our business attire so we could go to a park. Of course, we chose Magic Kingdom. We put on some shorts and, of course, our new mouse ears, and hopped onto the first Magic Kingdom area bus that pulled up. I say Magic Kingdom *area*, because getting to the Magic Kingdom as a CP on the Transtar buses can be involved. Transtar, the company that runs the CP buses (though I really wish they were run by Disney), only stops at Disney University/West Clock. Disney University is down the road from the Magic Kingdom and West Clock is the backstage area of the park where Cast Members who work there would go to park their cars and enter the Utilidors. There is a separate (Disney operated) shuttle bus that goes from the parking lot at Disney University to West Clock, although this is still unhelpful if you are visiting the park as a guest because you need to enter through the guest entrance if you are not working.

Although there is no direct bus between CP housing and Magic Kingdom, there are a number of ways to get to the park from there as a guest. A lot of CPs take the Transtar bus to the Contemporary and walk to the Magic Kingdom. I've done this a couple of times; it's a short walk, but it's annoying to be dropped off and have that "so close, yet so far" feeling. Another way to get to Magic Kingdom is to take the CP bus to the TTC (Transportation and Ticket Center) and take a monorail to the park. (This is what we did on that first day. It worked out fine, especially if you enjoy taking the monorail.) Usually, however, I take the CP bus to the Polynesian and get on the monorail from there. I love walking around the shops at the Polynesian, and this method allows me to get food from Kona Café to go that I can bring back to my apartment.

When the four of us arrived at the park that day, we had no idea how to get in as guests with our new IDs. We knew they would not scan at the turnstiles, unlike a ticket or a MagicBand, so we asked one of the Cast Members working at the front entrance what we should do. We were directed to Guest Relations, where we showed our IDs and our licenses, and were then let into the park through a gate to the left of the Guest Relations kiosk outside the park. Essentially, we just walked right into the Magic Kingdom. It was a weird experience. To our left, we saw crowds of guests waiting in line to scan their tickets and MagicBands, and here we were on the other side of this unassuming gate next to Guest Relations.

Ordinarily, during my first visit to the Magic Kingdom of each Disney trip, I look at how the train station at the front entrance is decorated and grab a map and a Times guide to plan out my day. But this time, we were all just so excited to be there that we rushed through the gate and down Main Street, U.S.A. The Festival of Fantasy parade was just finishing as we arrived, and the music and atmosphere of the parade added even more to the experience we'd had that day in Traditions and now our "first" time in the Magic Kingdom. As the parade ended, we all agreed that we needed to avoid the herd of people who exit the park after the parade, so we ducked right into the Town Square Theater to meet Tinkerbell, who only had a 10-minute wait.

I had never been to any of the meet and greets inside the Town Square Theater, so I was excited to see what it was like. It was beautifully decorated inside, similar to the restaurant next door. To meet Tinkerbell, we would need to shrink down to her size. We did this with the help of a Character Attendant Cast Member, who brought us into a hallway where the walls around us began to change and we shrunk down to Tinkerbell's size. In the next room, we met Tinkerbell herself, standing among human-size objects such as books, cherries, and thimbles, all of which were now larger than us.

After meeting Tinkerbell, it finally began to set in that we were going to be here for five months. We spent the rest of the day going on rides and people-watching, and then had dinner at one of my favorite quick service restaurants, Columbia Harbour House.

As much as I would have loved to stay in the park to see Wishes that night, we left after dinner because we all needed to be up super early again the next day, surprise, surprise.

The day after Traditions, August 8, was our Welcome to Operations class. This class also took place at Disney University and started promptly at 7:30 am, meaning I had to be at the bus stop by 6:30, meaning I had to be awake by 5:00. At this point, I was already looking forward to my next day off so I wouldn't need to go outside while it was still dark.

I'm not quite sure how to describe Welcome to Operations. Overall, I was interested in all of the Disney training classes because I knew it would be a great experience to learn how a company like Disney trains its Cast Members to be the best in their fields. The class started on a high note—well, it did once we'd finished watching the obligatory safety video that we'd all seen three times by now. We watched another "Welcome to the Team" sort of video that was focused on Operations. In Disney terms, Operations is any role where you're out in the park working with guests and helping everything function the way it's supposed to.

After the video, the true tone of the class set in: safety, safety, and more safety. Saying that Disney takes safety seriously is an understatement. I do not think I'm capable of adequately explaining how important safety is for the Disney Company. Everywhere you go backstage there are signs telling you not to text and drive (or walk) and little sayings like "Safe D begins with me". The first portion of the entire class on safety was boring, though completely necessary for working in any theme park. We watched a video that told us all about how evacuating the parks works, and different circumstances when the park would need to be evacuated. For instance, when the parks closed on 9/11, Cast Members made a chain by linking arms with each other to move guests toward the front of the park to exit. This is because the events of 9/11 did not take place in the parks, so there was no reason to have guests exit through backstage areas. If the situation was not 9/11, but rather a fire in the park that might block off Main Street, guests would be taken through a backstage area to exit. If the situation was an immediate threat, such as gunmen or terrorists, then leaving the park in any kind of an organized manner would be impossible, and so the protocol (as would be expected) is to take cover with whatever you can and encourage guests to do the same. Disney categorizes these scenarios into Evacuation plans A, B, and C.: Plan A is "as usual" (exit through the front gates), Plan B is "next best" (exit through back stage), and Plan C is "take cover".

We then learned how we should assist guests with disabilities. Disney is huge on treating each guest like an individual, and with the utmost respect, so we always say "guest with disabilities", not "disabled guest", because the person comes before the disabilities. We were told about the various disability services offered by Disney, and how we could access them if necessary.

This portion of the class, though boring compared to our previous training, was obviously very important. The next two hours of the class, however, were unbearable. While I'm sure the state of exhaustion we were in did not help, I have never been so bored in my life. Watching grass grow or paint dry would have been more entertaining than the next part of Welcome to Operations.

After a quick break, we were presented with a 64-slide PowerPoint presentation that would last the duration of the class. The point of the presentation was to teach us the safest ways of performing physically laborious tasks at work. Whether or not this actually helps, I'm not entirely sure; I don't ever think about it if I'm in my green zone when I'm lifting merchandise, and I never find myself in any kind of physical pain anyway. The presentation essentially taught us different ways of lifting, bending, and turning, to put the least amount of stress on our bodies. Each slide was read to us via recording by the most monotone voice I've ever heard, while a figure on the screen slowly demonstrated the specific motion. It was literally 64 slides of: "When lifting a box, remain in your green zone. Hold your elbows close to your shoulders, and bend the knees slightly. Lifting your arms too much will cause you to go into your yellow or red zones, which can cause injury." There were also times where the instructor made us stand up and act out the poses. Can you imagine how stupid a group of college students decked out in business attire and running on 3 hours sleep look while picking up imaginary boxes in slow motion? Well, I can, and we looked pretty ridiculous. Now, whenever someones (sarcastically or not), says, "Stay in your green zone!" at work I cringe.

After that draining experience, I went home and took the most glorious nap I have ever taken. Later on that day, I went to Epcot with Paulina and Lexie. We rode Spaceship Earth and Maelstrom, and spent some time in World Showcase. We stayed for Illuminations, since we finally had a night where we could stay up and not have to get up so early the next morning. Of course, I fell asleep on the bus ride home and managed to sleep for a few extra hours by the pool at our apartment the next morning as well.

On that day, August 9, Lexie and I were both off, so we spent the day in Animal Kingdom. One of the places we visited was DinoLand U.S.A., where I would be working. We rode DINOSAUR and spent some time in Chester and Hester's stupid carniv—I mean Dino-Rama, where we played the games and met Anthony, one of my future coworkers. Anthony was part of the Fall Advantage College Program. He had arrived in May, and so he had already been working in DinoLand all summer. I asked him how he liked working there and he said it was fine. It was not his first choice for a location either, but it was easy and the games were not as bad as he thought they would be. I was still not looking forward to running carnival games, but he did make me feel a little bit better about it. I ended up winning a prize on Mammoth Marathon, the game he was running. We went home with a small pink dinosaur that would sit in our apartment and be named Anthony. It was funny at the time, but now it seems a little creepy. Anthony, if you're reading this, don't think we're creepy; we just needed a name for the dinosaur.

On Sunday, August 10, I was up bright and early again for my first day in Animal Kingdom. No matter where you work in Disney, your first day is a general orientation of your area, be it a park, resort, water-park, Downtown Disney, or a backstage location. Because I was placed in Animal Kingdom, my orientation began at Animal Kingdom's Cast Services building. My orientation class was called DAKlimation (DAK being Disney's Animal Kingdom). DAKlimation was my first time going backstage in Animal Kingdom, and it was interesting to see how everything looked from behind the scenes. When I got off the bus near the park entrance, in my not-so-weather-appropriate business attire, I turned left to go toward the entrance of the Cast Member parking lot. Beyond that entrance is two crosswalks that bring Cast Members behind the park to a zoom gate, where you must tap your company ID against a scanner to gain access to the revolving door that lets you out backstage. After passing through the door, we waited for another bus to take us to the Cast Services building. (This was not a CP bus, but rather a Cast Member bus for anyone who works in Animal Kingdom.)

The bus dropped us off at the Cast Cafeteria, known as Pride Rock. It's catered by Sodexo and has a wide variety of food including a salad bar, fresh fruit, an international station, grill station, grab-and-go station, and a Subway. In this same building is the learning resource center for Animal Kingdom where Cast Members can use computers, take out books, and even use Rosetta Stone software for free. There is also a station where you can get new pins for Cast Member lanyards (though I've never once gotten pins from there because I work on the other side of the park and going to Pride Rock to get new pins isn't worth the time it would take me to get there).

We walked by Pride Rock toward the Cast Services building, where we were to meet the instructor for DAKlimation in the lobby. On the way, I saw some unused floats from the old Jammin' Jungle Parade and some safari trucks. Outside of Cast Services, there is also the safari truck with the Audio-Animatronic elephant Little Red, who used to be at the end of the safari ride. Her head still moves and the audio still comes from the truck, so it was cool to be able to see that since I remember it so well from the original version of the ride.

After waiting for a couple of minutes inside the lobby of Cast Services, we were greeted by our instructor and taken to a classroom. No one was excited to watch the same exact safety video about evacuating the building again, but of course it needed to be done in order for class to start. As before, we got another welcome video, with various Animal Kingdom Cast Members welcoming us to their park. Following the video, we learned about how Animal Kingdom is different from other Disney theme parks. The focus of this portion of the class was on how the park maintains its membership within the AZA (Association of Zoos and Aquariums) and how the Disney Worldwide Conservation Fund works to save animals all over the world. Learning about the conservation fund was extremely interesting because I did not entirely know all of the specifics about it when I had visited the park as a guest in the past. I knew that the money in the fund went directly to different sources, but I didn't know much about those sources. It turns out they can be anything from education, for teaching students how to act responsibly to save their environment, or for countries where poaching threatens endangered animals and the local population is unaware of how to handle it. A lot of the money also goes toward disaster relief, such as helping animals after events like hurricanes or oil spills. The really neat part of the Disney Worldwide Conservation Fund is that Disney covers all overhead costs and matches each donation. So if you were to donate $5 to the fund, Disney would also donate $5, and none of that money would go toward paying office staff, accountants, or travel bills. Disney covers all of those extra costs, and the entire $10 would be sent directly to the organization in need.

Moving on from the DWCF, we were instructed to look at the objects on the table in front of us, and to think about how we might come across these objects while working in the park. Some of the objects were obvious, such as maps and celebration buttons, and some were not, such as a mound of dirt or mud.

We then walked back over to Pride Rock as a group where we ate lunch before heading off to our tour of the park. Everyone at my table had Subway, probably because we didn't really know what Sodexo had to offer and no one wanted to look like a newbie in front of all the regular Cast Members. When we left Pride Rock, we were shown the "proper" way to walk around backstage, which is in the crosswalk at all times, no matter the circumstances. I'm pretty sure that the road we crossed was closed due to construction, but remember, safe D begins with me, so in the crosswalk we went.

We entered the park through a backstage gate across from Pride Rock that led us into Harambe, the village in the Africa portion of the park. First on our agenda was to ride Kilimanjaro Safari as a group! We were taken through the exit of the ride and then backstage, where we bypassed the 60-minute wait and had a safari truck all to ourselves. *How many people can say they went on an African safari as part of their training?* The safari was fun and a great way to start off our tour of the park. I would have loved to take pictures on it, but no one else had their phones or cameras out, so I wasn't sure if it would be okay. Generally, you cannot use any kind of electronic device while you're on the clock. Since we were on the road while technically working for Disney, I figured that taking pictures would be a bad idea.

After our safari, the heat and humidity began to set in, and we all began to regret our business attire. The rest of the day's schedule included a tour of the entire park, which was extremely interesting, but also extremely uncomfortable. I loved learning about the planning and design stages of each area of the park, but I felt disgusting in my pencil skirt and blazer, and the flats I was wearing were not the proper shoes in which to be walking around Animal Kingdom.

About halfway through the tour, while we were leaving Asia, I met Josh, another DinoLand CP. It was about time I met someone else from my area. He mentioned how I was only the second person he met from DinoLand, and he felt the same way as I did—that it would be difficult to meet many people working in an area with so few Cast Members. As we passed through the DinoLand portion of our tour and saw the costumes the Cast Members wear in Chester and Hester's Dino-Rama, we both cringed and dreaded going to Costuming later that day to pick up and try on our costumes for the first time. Josh also said that he was not excited to be running the carnival games in Chester and Hester's, so at least I wasn't at the only one to feel that way.

When we finished the tour of the park, we returned to our classroom inside the Cast Services building and were greeted by the best feeling in the world: air conditioning. The couple of hours that we had just spent in the park were entirely outdoors, and the whole experience was uncomfortable due to the ridiculous heat and humidity. Back in the classroom, we were asked to describe the objects on the tables in front of us, which we were all able to do except for the little mud piles. Everyone described them as mud, but little did we know they were actually preserved pieces of animal poop. Luckily, I hadn't touched them.

On that note, we were off to Costuming.

Going to a Disney Costuming building for the first time is overwhelming. We took a bus to Animal Kingdom's Costuming, or "Wardrobe Issue" as the sign outside states. The other parks all have their Costuming centers backstage somewhere, so Animal Kingdom is kind of a pain in that it is a separate bus ride away from the rest of the park. Once inside, we were in a state of shock at the size and scope of the facility. There were racks upon racks upon racks of costumes for Animal Kingdom as well as for Animal Kingdom Lodge. Before we went off in search of our costumes, our DAKlimation instructor gave us a word of warning: the sizes of Disney costumes are not generous to females. We were told to take no offense to the size that our costumes would be, and that the easiest way to figure out our Disney pants size would be to take our regular pants size and double it, and use that size as a basis for trying costumes on. So if you're a size 10 in your everyday jeans, and you want to come work for Disney, be prepared to try on pants that are a size 20.

Because we were all working in different areas of the park, and would therefore need different costumes, we were left to our own devices, and had to divide and conquer the building. One good thing was that it allowed me to meet other DinoLand Cast Members, finally, as it was clear who was working there by what aisle they were searching through. At Costuming that day I met Margaret and Sammie, two more DinoLand Merchandise CPs, and they weren't thrilled by their costumes or work location, either.

Animal Kingdom's Quick Service Cast Members have some of the worst Disney costumes I've ever seen, but as far as Merchandise goes, the Chester and Hester costume for DinoLand has them beat. The shorts are lime green with orange dinosaur prints and bright red dinosaur footprints on the thighs. Some of the shorts even have the red dino prints on the back pockets—talk about an awkward location! The shirts are bowling style, also bright red, with a small Chester and Hester's logo, but also three oversized buttons we have to pin on with tacky sayings like "Dino Discounts, Bargain Bones!" and "We Dig Dinos!" There is an optional blue hat that hardly anyone wears. Costuming was out of the blue hats that first day I went, and I never did come back for one. I don't think this monstrosity needs anymore accessories. The shorts also need to be worn on your natural waist, not on your hips and tucked in. And the shirts that claim to be "women's" in Disney Costuming are most definitely just men's shirts that have been moved under the sign reading "Female". I had to go up two sizes for the Chester shirts to button over my chest, and the shirts make the shape of my body look so much like a barrel that tucking my shirt in and pulling my shorts up to my natural waist actually helped the situation.

Thankfully, no matter how bad your Disney costume seems, it really isn't that bad. It's *terrible* the first time you try it on in Costuming, but not that terrible when you wear it to work and it blends it with the scenery and everyone else is wearing the same thing. The only really aggravating thing about my first Chester costume had to do with my shorts, but that was my own fault. I was sweaty, tired, and sick of running back and forth in my business attire between the dressing room and the rack. Even though I was told to double my pants size, I had too much pride to actually do this, so I began by trying on shorts that were a size 14, my regular non-Disney pants size. They barely got over my hips, so I went back to the rack and grabbed a 16...then an 18...then a 20. Fed up with the rate I was going (which was entirely my own fault),I grabbed three size 28s off the rack and called it a day with the Chester costume. Of course, these shorts were huge, and Anthony affectionately referred to them as my gangster shorts for the first week or so until I went back to Costuming for new ones. (I soon learned that my true Disney size is a 22. So if I had just tried on one more size instead of grabbing the 28s out of frustration, I could have avoided a week in gangster shorts.)

For DinoLand Merchandise, we have 3 costumes: the Chester atrocity, the Dino Institute outfit, and the floor stock costume, which every Animal Kingdom Merchandise Cast Member wears for floor stock shifts. The only costumes I received that day were the Chester costume and the Dino Institute costume. The Dino Institute costume isn't bad; it's the same one that Attractions Cast Members wear at the DINOSAUR ride, and rather plain but surprisingly flattering as far as Disney costumes go. My only complaint is that I have pleated pants with mine, because Costuming is always out of Dinosaur pants in my size and Custodial pants are the backup.

I asked one of the Costuming Cast Members if I was all set or if I needed a third costume before I left for the day. She said I was all set.

I responded with, "Are you sure? Because I talked to one of my coworkers yesterday and he said I would need a floor stock costume."

"Nope, you're all set."

I was not all set. If you're reading this and you're planning on doing the program, take this advice: the people who work in Costuming never seem to actually know anything about the costumes. If you have a question about your costume, ask someone at your work location, not someone from Costuming. I had to get up two hours earlier for my floor stock training shift to go to Costuming and get a floor stock costume since I did not get it during DAKlimation, even though I knew I needed it. The Cast Members at Costuming also did not tell me that I should get rain gear on my first day there, which left me with the impression that I would get it from my work location. I didn't know I needed to go to Costuming for a poncho and a pouch to keep it in until I was stuck at a merchandise cart during a sun shower my first week without a trainer.

Another word of advice: if you need shoes for your costume, you can get them at Magic Kingdom Costuming and have the money taken out of your paycheck, which seems easier than trekking over to Wal-Mart for a pair of work shoes. I brought work shoes with me, but I went with a friend to get hers from Costuming and it was very convenient, especially if you don't have a car.

Chapter Ten

Get a good idea and stay with it. Do it and work at it until it's done right.

Merchandise Tier 1 was the first on-the-job training I had during my program. This day, as per usual for Disney's training schedule, started bright and early at the Cast Services building backstage in Animal Kingdom. When I got off the bus with the other new CPs at Animal Kingdom, we were still unsure where to go. Even though we were just there for DAKlimation, learning your way around Disney's backstage areas takes some time. Thankfully, another CP who had been there longer than us knew exactly where we needed to go and showed us the way. When we arrived at Cast Services, we again waited in the lobby, similar to DAKlimation. The lobby of Cast Services is where I met a lot of fellow CPs who worked in Animal Kingdom. We were all awkwardly stuck there waiting for class during those first couple of days, so we became close even though we all worked in different lands throughout the park. Finally, a trainer came out to the lobby to greet us and bring us to where we would clock in.

Clocking in, though it sounds simple, was not so simple to learn while I was training. When our day started at the Cast Services building, we would "wall clock in", something we would never do when we were actually on the job. To wall clock in (or out), you simply slide your company ID through a device that is attached to a wall, and then press "in" or "out". When you are actually on the job after your training is finished, you clock in using the CDS, but I'll explain that later.

Our Tier 1 training began in a room filled with computers, where we completed a painfully boring e-learning program about the Disney Dining Plans. This may have been painfully boring for me because I was already familiar with the different plans (or maybe it was because the program itself was dull). The program explained the different plans and food options to us, and culminated with a short quiz. The dining plans are not actually that important for day-to-day Merchandise. The only part of the dining plan we deal with is the snack credit, usually in the form of a bottle of soda or small snack like a Mickey rice krispies treat—basically whatever snack items can be sold in gift shops. When we finished the quiz, we were told to raise our hand and someone would come over to help us. I was the first person to raise my hand, and upon showing one of the trainers my completed quiz screen, I was taken to a table in the back of the room.

At the table I met "Bill", who I was told would be my trainer (at least for that day.) Bill was helpful and polite, but, as I would learn, he was a bit more strict than the other trainers. I would also learn that often there are more trainees with one trainer. That wasn't the case with me, as (except for my last day) I had Bill all to myself. I was happy for that, on the one hand, because the training was more personalized and I wasn't sharing my time with anyone else, but it also would have been nice to bond with another CP during training and to have someone to discuss it with besides Bill.

Before we left that room, Bill gave me a sheet of paper with a personality test on it. The test was meant to determine how I learned best. Kudos to Disney for trying to individualize the training process; that was definitely something different that I haven't seen other companies doing. My test concluded that I learn best from reading and trying things myself. I could have told them that, but I thought it was neat how Disney (and Disney trainers) go the extra mile.

Once that was over, Bill gave me my pin lanyard. Pin trading is a huge part of working in Merchandise, and it quickly became one of my favorite things to do at work. In addition to the lanyard itself and my twelve starter pins, he also gave me a little brochure with some rules about pin trading. The rules were basic, though Bill went into detail about them. He said that I needed to have twelve pins on the lanyard at all times, and that a guest could not trade with me more than twice. I know that this is technically a rule of pin trading, but I'm pretty sure no one follows it, especially if the guest is a child. He also said that this was a work lanyard and that the pins were not to go into my personal collection. This is another rule that most Cast Members break. If they are traded a pin they like, chances are it goes right into their pockets and is quickly replaced by a trader pin of their own that they want to get rid of.

Learning about pin trading was my first clue that Bill was a strict trainer. At first, I would never trade pins from my work lanyard, because it was engrained into my mind that it was a bad idea, and it was against the rules, but all of my coworkers did it all the time as if were nothing. Bill, however, was really into this rule, even if no one else was too concerned about it. Bill also taught me the proper way to hold out my pin lanyard so that guests wouldn't be staring at my chest while looking at them. I (perhaps immaturely) found this conversation kind of funny, because you could tell that he was very uncomfortable discussing the matter. He told me that because I was a lady, I would want to hold my pins up away from my chest when people ask if they can see them. Apparently, guests can get grabby while looking at pins, and Disney does not want any funny business to happen while we're working.

After we finished our discussion about pin trading, we moved on to the four keys...again. This is when it became clear that I was with the strictest trainer ever. As I looked at the other CPs sitting with their trainers, I saw them idly chatting and relaxing. Not Bill; he was grilling me on the Four Keys. This exchange was awkward— not because I didn't know the Four Keys (by this point I knew them inside and out); it was awkward because no one else was being asked about them. Bill was the only trainer who asked Four Keys-related questions while we were sitting at the table, leading me to believe that I was in for a rough day. The questions he asked were not difficult, they were mostly "What are the Four Keys?" "Give me an example of safety." or "Give me an example of show." I was just confused about why they were being asked. He was not taking notes, but it felt more like an interview and less like an ordinary conversation, so at the time I wasn't quite sure what all of these questions were about.

Something very exciting, and very important, happened next: Bill took out a little red "Earning My Ears" ribbon and attached it to my nametag. I was finally, *officially*, earning my ears.

Moving on from our Q&A session, we headed toward Pride Rock for lunch. I didn't realize it at the time, but I should have valued my meals at Pride Rock while I was training, because there was no way I'd be back there once I started working. DinoLand is on the opposite end of the park, and I would have spent my whole break getting back and forth. Lunch was sufficiently awkward because our trainers ate with us, and it was clear that the CPs did not know how to act around them. I can honestly say that on that first day I didn't understand the hierarchy of Merchandise trainers. For all I knew, they could have been our direct managers, so everyone was quiet while they ate, making for a slightly uncomfortable meal. As it turns out, they are just Merchandise trainers, who we would not see again once we finished training, unless we saw them helping someone else "earn their ears".

When lunch was over, Bill took me to DinoLand.

"Finally," I thought...a thought that would become a common thread throughout training. Any CP will tell you that training to work at Disney is a long, grueling process. While some of the training was fun and entertaining, the process was long, and we all quickly reached the point where we just wanted to be done and working on our own. I had not reached that point yet, but I did want to get out of the classroom and into DinoLand. I had now been there for over a week, and this was only the second time I'd been in my park.

Once we reached DinoLand, I was hoping that Bill would teach me its back story. In my own opinion, DinoLand is an eyesore to Walt Disney World. I have always found the carnival atmosphere to be tacky, and not something you'd expect to see, or want to see, in a Disney park. Because of this, I was curious to learn more of the back story. (Maybe there's a part of the story I'm missing here. Maybe they'll teach me about it, and this place will all make sense. Maybe I won't think it's tacky anymore. Or maybe it really is the tacky mess I always thought it was, and I'll be spending the next five months as a glorified carny.) Bill did not tell me the details of DinoLand U.S.A. and why Chester and Hester's mess of a carnival sideshow exists. Instead, we walked right into the biggest gift shop in DinoLand, where I would be spending much of my time working: Chester and Hester's Dinosaur Treasures. I stood next to Bill as we walked in, expecting him to give me a tour of the space, since I'd be working here for five months. Instead of a tour or even an overview of the shop, we went right through a door labeled "shopkeepers only" that opened up into the stockroom.

Inside the stockroom was a CDS computer (where I would clock in and get my assignments once I was finished training) and the money room. The door exiting the stockroom, toward the back of the building, led to an outdoor stock area with a roof over it. And down a small hill from there was a trailer where I would take my breaks. Bill knocked on the door of the money room, and one of the managers, "Anna", came over to greet us.

Bill left me with Anna, who brought me into the money room and introduced herself to me and welcomed me to the DinoLand family.

After asking a couple of basic questions, such as what school I went to, what I majored in, and so forth, she abruptly stated, "So now we're going to have you get out into the store and practice talking to strangers."

Excuse me?

"Okay..."

"It sounds weird to say it like that, but that's really what a lot of working here is about. You need to feel comfortable going up to people you don't know and starting conversations."

Okay, that makes sense, I guess.

"So we're going to have you go out into the store, and I'll stay close by to kind of watch how you're doing. This way you can practice interacting with guests."

So that's it? I've been in this store for all of three minutes, and you're just going to throw me out there to talk to guests?

"It's not as awkward as it sounds, and talking to guests is one of the best parts of working in Merchandise."

Says you, who has been in this store for more than three-and-a-half minutes...

So I went out into the store, with Anna close behind, and began talking to guests. This whole situation was odd to me. I didn't have any idea what to say. And if anyone asked me a question, I most likely would not know the answer, since I had hardly spent time in the store and I knew almost nothing about it.

"Do you sell Minnie ears in here?"

"Umm, I think so." I quickly scanned the entire store, "Oh, yes! We do! They're right over here."

Phew. Thank God there are some things that are inevitably sold at almost any Disney gift shop.

I had no idea what to say to guests in a place that I was completely unfamiliar with, so I simply asked how they were doing. They all either answered with "good" or did not answer at all.

"So you're doing great so far, but..." Anna began.

There's already a "but"?

"We really want to make sure that we're asking our guests more open-ended questions. Asking how their day is going or if they need help finding anything is okay, but it would be better to ask a question that allows us to get to know more about them. Try asking who they're shopping for, or where they're from, for instance."

Was this a test? Why was this happening?

I went back into the shop and asked a couple who they were shopping for, and they told me about their daughter back in England who loved Stitch. They were looking at the Stitch plushes, but mentioned that they would not want to carry it around the park all day. I found out that they were staying at a Disney resort, so I told them that we offered complimentary shipping to their resort; that way they wouldn't need to carry it around the park all day.

Anna was impressed by this conversation, enough so that I was put out of my misery and brought back to Bill. I don't mean to make it sound like training was horrible, because it really wasn't, I just don't understand why I was thrown into it like that. Later in the week I talked to other CPs, and apparently this didn't happen to anyone else, so I'm not sure why it happened to me. I think that one way or another it was Bill's doing, since no other DinoLand CP had been asked to randomly talk to strangers without first having learned anything about their location.

Before leaving the shop, Bill pointed out a photo hanging on the wall.

"There they are," he said, "Chester and Hester."

I looked at the photo, perplexed by the couple, er, siblings, er... man and woman's faces.

"Do they have the same face on different bodies?" I asked.

Bill just laughed and led the way outside.

"What are the Four Keys?"

"Safety, Show, Courtesy, Efficiency."

"Give me an example of safety."

"Making sure guests always wear shoes."

"Good."

We walked by the crocodile located in DinoLand, which Bill said would be a great thing to point out to guests. I thought this was really cool, because I never even noticed that there was a crocodile in DinoLand (probably because I avoided DinoLand.) I always thought of DinoLand as the one part of Animal Kingdom without any actual animals, but there are a couple—a crocodile and a tortoise—both right near Chester and Hester's.

"Alright, so I'm giving you a challenge," Bill said.

Didn't I have enough of a challenge in the gift shop back there?

"We're going to walk through the entire park, and along the way you need to perform five instances of the Four Keys."

I'm sure Bill meant well, but I really did not like how everything was a "challenge" on my first day. Thankfully, this challenge was much easier than the whole "Talk to people you don't know, about products you don't know, in the store you don't know" thing.

I got Courtesy out of the way twice, right off the bat. I offered to take a photo for a family so they could all be in it, and I got down to a child's level to pin trade with him. Safety was pretty easy, too: I told a couple of kids to stop running and checked that one off the list. Show and Efficiency were more difficult to accomplish, since I wasn't actually working yet. By this point we were in Asia, so if anything, I was taking away from the show by walking around that land in my DinoLand costume. Eventually, I completed the challenge and was brought back to Cast Services, where I was released for the day.

The next day, August 12, 2014, was my Merchantainment class, back at Disney University. This was where we would learn how to use the cash register. The classroom was kind of funny looking, because half of the room had regular chairs and the other half was filled with counters to stand behind with registers on them so we could all practice. This made a lot more sense than having us learn the register on the job; given how busy Disney gift shops are, guests would be very annoyed with new people on the registers.

The register portion of the class was straightforward. The POS system was similar to that used by other retailers, though surprisingly unsophisticated for what I would have expected to find at Disney. (For instance, if someone was using a Cast Member discount and they bought a t-shirt and a DVD, we would have to ring the products up separately, because there is no Cast Member discount on DVDs, but the register isn't smart enough to only discount one item in the transaction.) When I worked at Staples, the register would have been able to handle something like that, and you'd think that Disney's POS system would be even more advanced and user friendly.

We also learned how to count change back to guests the Disney way. Counting change the Disney way means counting up while placing the money in the guest's hand. So if I'm ringing you out, and your total comes to $3.70, and you hand me a $5 bill, I'm supposed to count your change aloud like so, while handing it back to you: "$3.70, $.30

makes it $4.00, and $1 makes $5 total. Have a magical day!" (Or "wild time" I guess, since I'd be working in Animal Kingdom.) Counting up isn't what's confusing—it's just confusing when there is a screen in front of you telling you what the change is, and yet you need to count up when giving the change back to the guest.

The only time I counted change back the Disney way was during this class, and I have yet to see anyone else count this way. It takes up too much time at the end of a transaction when the guest is clearly done being in a gift shop. During my my Tier 3 training, I learned that Bill, who was so enthralled by all of Disney's rules, did not make me count change back the Disney way. As long as I told guests how much change they'd be receiving as I handed it to them, he was pleased enough.

Also in our Merchantainment class, we watched some videos that showed us other Cast Members merchantaining, or entertaining with the merchandise. This would be one of the more fun (and easy) parts of our job, and we were all looking forward to it.

Lastly, we were told the importance of being trustworthy, since we would be responsible for large sums of cash. We also watched videos that made clear we were always on camera, and if we took any money out of the register we'd caught. After watching footage of former Cast Members stealing money, we returned to the POS a final time for a role-play activity. Each of us was given a card with a scenario on it, something like "You are paying for a Tigger plush with $20 in cash, $20 on a gift card, and the rest on a credit card", and we acted as guests for each other so we could practice the more "complicated" transactions. We also learned to rip receipts in half if guests do not want to take them, so that if they were to end up on the floor no one can pick them up and try to get away with a fraudulent return.

August 13, 2014, was my Tier 3 Merchandise training day. (If you're confused about where Tier 2 went, don't worry, I was confused, too. Tier 2 is the Merchantainment class, though at the time many of us wondered if we somehow we had missed our Tier 2 class.) Tier 3 meant that I was finally going to be on the register, in my location, with real guests. *No more classrooms and role-play activities—finally!*

I was paired up with Bill again, and up bright and early, as my training was scheduled from 7:00 am to 2:30 pm. The park opened at 8:00 am for Extra Magic Hours that day, so Bill and I were able to attend the morning meeting in Chester's. The meeting was run by whichever leader was the opening manager for our location that morning. He or she would tell us if there was any news about the company as a whole, or our specific area, that we needed to know about. The next topics would usually include things we were doing well and things that needed to be improved, and of course, there was a heavy focus on the Four Keys. Before the meeting concluded, the manager would ask if anyone else had anything to add, and if we had any good Four Keys-related stories to share. Sometimes the stories included magical moments Cast Members had performed the day before, and sometimes they would be something like "I noticed I child climbing on the dinosaur outside, so I told him to get down." The first kind of story is an example of a worthwhile story, something was actually good enough to be shared during a meeting. The latter is an example of a Cast Member realizing that no one else was going to speak up, and the manager would not be happy until someone shared a story.

After the meeting, Bill and I went to open the Boneyard Cart. This cart is immediately next to the Boneyard attraction, and the merchandise there includes dinosaur eggs, that hatch when placed in water, t-shirts, hats, latex dinosaurs, dinosaur pinchers, tote bags, drinks, and cooling fans, among a couple of other items. This is generally the quietest cart in DinoLand, and most of the cart's business seems to be from guests purchasing water bottles and coke as they walk by on hot days. Opening the cart was extremely straightforward—pull the ropes to lift up the tarps and tie them on the sides, uncover the drinks, make sure all the merchandise looks neat and ready to go, and unroll the coins in the register. When I open a cart in the morning, a manager has already unlocked the bottom of the tarp and placed the cash drawer into the register (but they don't unroll the coins for us). Disney does not allow us to bang the rolls of coins off the counter, so Bill told me that it is helpful to unroll them when you open in the morning so that you're not stuck trying to unroll them during your first transaction.

Bill rang out the first transaction for me, and after that, it was my turn. I felt pretty confident on the register; it was easy to use during Merchantainment, and I've worked retail so often that there wasn't anything POS-related that I was worried about. Another guest came to the cart and handed me a slip of paper with $80 written on it in permanent marker. I looked at Bill, confused, who explained that guests who are getting caricatures done are given those slips from the vendor (who is third party and not affiliated with Disney) so that we can ring them up on the register. I found the button on the screen labeled "caricature" and typed in the amount on the slip, $80. The total amount came out to more than $80, which angered the guest. Bill explained that there is a sales tax, while the guest argued that he was paying for a service and not a product and therefore there should be no tax. Bill apologized for the confusion and explained that Guest Relations could better help him out. The guest was still unhappy, but took his change and left to get his caricature done, regardless. This was the first and only time I've had someone question the sales tax on the price for their caricature. They're not providing a service, they're selling a product. Face painting in the parks does not carry a sales tax.

The rest of the transactions I had on the register at the Boneyard Cart were uneventful. I did notice the music for DinoLand while I was there, something that I had never noticed in the past as a guest. The area music for DinoLand is a radio show with the Digger and Bonehead, who are interns for the Dino Institute (the scientific research facility where the DINOSAUR ride is located). They've taken over the airwaves to play dinosaur-related songs all day. Their radio show is complete with dinosaur puns and songs like "Bad to the Bone", and "Walk the Dinosaur". When I finally noticed the music, I thought that it was really cute and surprisingly well done. This was the first of many small details in DinoLand that I discovered only after having worked there, but not as a guest.

After about an hour on the Boneyard Cart, another DinoLand Cast Member came over and handed Bill a slip of paper. This is how Cast Members know where they're going next. One Cast Member logs into CDS on the computer to get their assignment. When his or her assignment prints out, it includes instructions for the Cast Member whose place is being taken as well. So the slip might say, "Amy, please go pickup Boneyard Cart (from Bill). Bill, please pickup Dino Cart (from Theresa). Theresa, please return to the PC for a new assignment." The slip of paper is handed off to the next Cast Member so that they know where to go next.

Bill and I were off to Dino Cart, which is up the small hill from the Boneyard Cart going toward the Discovery Island Bridge. At this point, I felt extremely comfortable with the register and opening carts, and ready to be on my own. Instead of being on my own, however, I was going to be spending the next five hours with Bill. I have nothing against Bill, though he was kind of strict at times; it wasn't him that I was tired of, it was the training. I felt as though the job itself was easy, and I was ready to be on my own.

Because it was still pretty slow, Bill showed me the merchandise at the Dino Cart and explained what we usually sell the most of there. The cart is split into three sections—Monsters University merchandise, plush, and shoes (primarily Crocs and Disney flip-flops). In addition, this cart had one specific task that the others lacked. At Dino Cart, I get to be a part of the Wilderness Explorers program, even though my role is Merchandise. The Wilderness Explorers program allows kids to join the same group that Russell from *Up* was a part of, while they go around the park completing activities and collecting badges. The signal flag badge is given out at Dino Cart. To complete the task and earn their badge, kids need to find three signal flags and point them out to me, and tell me which flags they are according to a list they have in their Wilderness Explorer books. The activity is very similar to something I'd be doing in the museum field if I were still working back home, so I felt comfortable with this task as well.

Bill explained that there was a joke I could use while running this activity. One of the flags has marshmallows on it, and unsurprisingly, this flag is the "S'mores Tonight" flag. When giving out the badges, I have the option of saying, "Do you know why they're called s'mores?" Then I wait a few beats and say, "Because after you have one, you always want s'more!" Bill liked the joke, so I said it while I was training, and a couple of times after, but it almost never got laughs, especially from kids. Sometimes the parents would laugh, like they knew I was trying and didn't want to be rude, but it usually did not receive the reaction that Bill hoped for. Now that I've finished training, I only say this joke when the moment seems right, and it seems like the guests in front of me will be receptive to it.

Throughout the rest of the day, Bill showed me the other places I could be working at in DinoLand. There were a few more carts. The Nemo cart is right outside the Theater in the Wild, where Finding Nemo: The Musical plays daily. As you'd expect, this cart primarily sells Nemo merchandise and drinks, and is only busy when the show gets out. Another cart in DinoLand is the Dino-Rama cart, located inside Chester and Hester's Dino-Rama, and selling primarily pins and tickets for the carnival games. On a busy day this cart gets crazy because so many people rush over to buy tickets with cash (as the games themselves can only take credit cards, gift cards, or MagicBands, and the Cast Members working the games don't want to be bothered with selling tickets). The last cart is the voucher cart, which is not a large kiosk-like cart that sells merchandise, but rather a literal cart that only sells games vouchers (or tickets; we use both terms interchangeably). This cart does not have an actual register, only a tablet with the POS loaded onto it and a cash drawer. On this cart, credit and cash transactions are run through the tablet and change is made with what is in the drawer. It is kind of like a cash apron, but not, because there is still a tablet where the tickets are rung up.

At the end of the day, Bill and I went into Chester and Hester's Dinosaur Treasures, the largest gift shop in DinoLand. The shop sells dinosaur merchandise as well as *Star Wars* and *Toy Story* products, and typical Disney gift shop items such as ear hats, plush, journals, and autograph books. There is also a candy section, which includes pucker powder sticks, bags for guests to fill with individually wrapped candy (which we weigh at the register), popcorn, and cookies. By the end of the day, working the register was a breeze; I just needed help every now and then when guests asked where merchandise was located, as I had only been in that store a couple of times.

Before clocking out for the day, Bill asked me if I had my floor stock costume all ready to go for the next day. *My floor stock costume? What?* I then learned that I needed to get yet another costume. Remember when I was in Costuming and I asked if I was all set? Well, I wasn't all set. Even though I was not scheduled until 11:30 am, and should have been able to sleep in a little bit, I needed to go back to Costuming to get my floor stock costume. Thankfully, this costume is very comfortable, and we don't need to tuck the shirt in. It's a mosaic, or giraffe-like printed shirt with khaki shorts.

Tier 4 Merchandise training, or floor stock, was not much different from Tier 3. I spent most of the day on the register again. The only floor stock-related part of my day was a pick list, which is a list of products that need to be stocked. You take the list to the stockroom with you and record how many of each product you put out. (Other retailers, like Staples, called this a pull list; it's the same thing.) Filling out the pick-list was easy, but monotonous to do while training.

For reasons that I don't understand, that is all the floor stock training we receive during Tier 4. It is not hard to pick up, but it is different in every location. In DinoLand, we check out keys from our managers, because some of the merchandise is located in carts that are locked, and we just go back and forth stocking whatever needs to be stocked all day.

Cast Members tend to either really like floor stock or really dislike it. I'm not a huge fan of it. I enjoy being on the register, where I'm busy and can talk to more people. During floor stock, I feel as though fewer guests talk to me, probably because I look busy, and they could talk to the person standing behind a register doing nothing instead. On the positive side, you pretty much run your floor stock shift the way you want to, and can take your breaks whenever you want, whereas with register shifts you need to wait for the CDS to tell you that it's time to go on break.

After a couple of days off, it was time for my Tier 5 training, my last training, *or so I thought.* Tier 5 was photo training, and it was also my first day with a trainer besides Bill, and with another trainee. As I would later learn, most new CPs are trained in groups, and it was unusual for me to have been alone until now. I enjoyed being with another CP (Margaret) for this training, because I hardly knew anyone who worked in DinoLand at that point. With Bill, it was like being a kid in school who didn't have a partner and so had to pair up with the teacher for an activity.

Photo training took place in the Dino Institute, the same building where DINOSAUR is located, so we learned how to search for, print, and sell on-ride photos to guests. We also learned how to link the photos to Memory Maker, the pre-purchased photo program guests can buy, as well as Attractions+, a card that allows guests to download all of their on-ride photos for a set price. Learning the photo software was easy, and Photo quickly became my favorite part of working in DinoLand. (And of course, photo is where we are scheduled the least.)

After my photo training was complete, I was told that I could finally remove the red "earning my ears" ribbon from my nametag. This would not last for long, though, as I would be trained on the carnival games the next week, and would be given a new, white "earning my ears" ribbon for that training. Though my schedule referred to Tier 5 as my "last day", it was certainly not. I had a couple of regular non-training register shifts before I was back in training mode again for the games.

Chapter Eleven

*Certainly we have all had great confidence at one time in our lives,
though most of us lose it as we grow older. Because of my work, I've
been lucky to retain a shred of this useful quality but sometimes, as I
look back on how tough things were, I wonder if I'd go through it again.*

Games training began, as most training days do, bright and early.
I was (finally) paired up with someone who actually worked in
DinoLand, and I was mildly excited to get training underway. Our
games training is split up into two days, so that one day we can be
there in the morning and learn how to open the games, and the next
day we can be there at the end of the day to close them.

Opening the games is easy. Many of them just need the tarp lifted
up, which you do by attaching a long pole to a hook on the upper
interior of the game and turning it until the tarp goes up. Closing is
just the opposite. Some of the games have balls that need to be put
into position, which is also extremely easy to do. The most difficult
game to open is Mammoth Marathon (the ski ball-esque game in the
back) because it takes three people to lift the heavy tables up or down.

The first game I was trained on was Brontoscore, a typical carni-
val-style basketball game. Guests can play individually, and the prizes
they get are based upon how many shots they make. I watched my
trainer interact with guests and run the game on the microphone
about three or four times. In that short period, I formed my first
impressions of all the DinoLand games. They weren't that bad. I could
not imagine loving them, but there are parts of every job that you
don't love. After observing my trainer, I was given the microphone
and told to give it a shot. *Already?! I don't know what I'm doing yet.*

Let me preface this by stating that public speaking is not my strong
suit. Have you seen *The Princess Diaries*? Do you remember the scene
where Mia is in debate class, and when she gets up to speak she runs
to the back of the room and vomits? That was me in high school,
complete with the school uniform, frizzy hair, and glasses. I was

literally Mia Thermopolis, and now here I am, running a carnival game on a microphone, with everyone focusing on me and whatever I'm saying. Nerve-wracking? What an understatement.

"So just make sure you interact with the guests and encourage them to come over here and play Brontoscore."

"Uh, hi, everyone. Come over here and play Brontoscore, it's uh... really fun...?"

Is that how my voice sounds? Do all microphones make your voice sound this weird? Maybe this mic is broken...

My trainer did not look impressed. He took the microphone back from me and demonstrated:

"Step right up! Grab some tickets and come on down to the Dino-Rama games! Tickets are 1 for $4, 3 for $10, or 5 for $15. Come right up to Brontoscore and win some prizes!"

I formed a new impression of the games: I don't like Chester and Hester's Dino-Rama. I don't like microphones. I *really* don't like the way my voice sounds on the microphone. And I don't like that whole continuously shouting at people until they come over thing.

When my trainer handed the microphone back to me, a father and son arrived with tickets in hand ready to play.

"Okay, I can take those tickets for you guys. So this is Brontoscore. If you get one ball in you get a small prize, two balls in you get a medium prize, and all three in you get the big prize."

After I handed the duo their prize, my trainer gave me some more advice:

"Don't call the balls 'balls'".

"Isn't that what they are?"

"Sometimes guests are very immature, so just cut that whole word out. 'One in gets a small prize, two in gets a medium prize...' like that."

Sure enough, I accidentally said the word "balls" to the next guy that played and he laughed. Men are so immature.

Before moving on to the next game, my trainer explained the importance of safety. Kids can only sit on the counters, not stand, and they must sit "crisscross apple sauce" with their parents standing directly behind them. (We can't say "Indian style" because that isn't PC.) And finally, they can only sit on the counter if their shoulder doesn't reach the counter. My trainer also mentioned that if kids do stand on the counters, or do anything that they're not supposed to, I would get in trouble. *So don't let that happen even if it's entirely out of my control? Ok...*

The next game was Wacky Packycephalosaur (aka Whack-a-mole), and this one required a lot more spieling:

"Welcome to Wacky Packycephalosaur, the more you hit the more you score! In front of you are some pachecephalosaurs, they have ten-inch thick skulls so you can whack them as hard as you want and they won't feel a thing! Each whack is ten points and the first player to 150 is our winner. Just make sure you only use your mallet, no hands and fingers—dinosaurs do bite. And you guys are going to be playing for the cotton candy chameleon!"

In addition to the spiel, we need to keep talking while they're playing:

"Keep whacking them! Whack 'em, whack 'em! Keep going, you guys are doing great!"

Until finally someone wins, and we look up at a screen to see which number won so we can give him or her a prize, while still encouraging everyone else who lost.

"And the winner is player four! Congratulations! Everyone else did great, too, thanks so much for playing, and have a wild day!"

Cue the tears. This is usually the time when at least one kid who didn't win cries. This wasn't an issue at Brontoscore, because as my trainer explained I would be in control of the game and I could give extra shots if I wanted to. But Wacky was a competition game, so there would only be one winner. *That's right, I go to work and make many children cry.*

There are a couple of tactics for fixing this situation, but they don't always work, and they're not always possible:

"Was that your first time playing? That was AMAZING for your first time! No one ever does that good the first time, great job!"

"But you already won that turtle, and everyone knows turtles are WAY COOLER than chameleons."

You could also let them play again for free, but this was also dependent on a couple of things. I didn't do it while I was with a trainer, because I wasn't sure if it was okay and didn't want to try it with someone there watching me. You also can't do that in front of certain management. Technically, it's not allowed, but in practice it's more of a "use your own judgment/don't overdo it" sort of a thing.

The last option is just to give a prize to the kid who cries, but I never do this, and my trainer also told me never to do it. I believe that giving a prize to a kid who lost a competition game and cries isn't teaching him anything, other than that crying will get them what they want. It's also not fair. I wouldn't be happy if I won, or if I was the parent of the kid who won, when anyone who cries gets a prize. More often, I would make it a tie if there are two siblings playing, because it's clear that one would freak out if he or she lost. This is still dependent on a couple of things—who is around at the time and what the stock of prizes is like: no one gets extra prizes if I'm running low on them and the stocker is nowhere to be found.

The next game I was trained on was Fossil Fueler. Running it is almost exactly the same as Wacky. Both games require you to kick on a switch in the ground for each person playing; the buttons to start the game and music work the same, as well. This is the game where you hold the gun and aim the stream of water at the target to win. But this is Disney, so we don't say "gun" or even "water".

"Welcome to Fossil Fueler! The goal of this game is to fill up your gas tank faster than the other players. To do this, simply aim your gas nozzle at the center dot in front of you. The fossil fuel will come out automagically, there are no buttons or switches to push. And the first player to fill up their tank will be taking home this sunburned Florida alligator! Are you all ready? Okay! Here we go!"

"Keep holding it! Hold it really steady! You guys are doing great!"

"And we have a winner right over on number six! Congratulations! Great job everyone, thanks so much for playing!"

Cue child crying.

I should also mention that there are nicknames we can call the prizes, or we can make up our own names for them as long as they're appropriate. The cotton candy chameleon I mentioned earlier is simply blue and pink, and the sunburned gator is red.

After my stint on Fossil, my first day of games training was over.

The next day I repeated Fossil and then went on to Mammoth Marathon and Comet Crasher. Mammoth Marathon can be my favorite and least favorite game to work. It's basically ski-ball combined with mammoths racing to get out of the Ice Age. The spiel has some terms to remember—it's not a glass panel, it's a "sheet of ice", and they're not balls (because we all know how inappropriate that would be), they're "snowballs". The game is fun because I like giving the commentary on the mammoths racing. You get to pretend you're an announcer at a race and keep track of who is in the lead, who is tied, and give your own little commentary on it. It was uncomfortable at first, but once I got used to speaking on the microphone it became a lot of fun. What is not fun about Mammoth is when guests expect you to sell them tickets while you're clearly spieling and trying to run a game. Unlike the other games, Mammoth has a cash register, so guests go there to buy tickets for *other* games. I'm usually pretty good at multitasking, and I've learned to spiel without watching how the race is going, so I can sell tickets at the same time, but it's still annoying. There are times when I'd like to be paying more attention to the race, but I can't because guests are hounding me to sell them tickets. Ideally, there would be two people working at Mammoth— one person to run the game and the other to sell tickets, though I don't think this will ever happen.

The other games do not have cash registers, only tablets, that have very slow Wi-Fi connections. Because of this, we can only take credit cards, gift cards, or MagicBands at the other games, and ringing them out is usually a slow process due to the tablets. It can be a hassle when you're also trying to run the game, so most Cast Members will send guests to the Dino-Rama cart, the voucher cart, or Mammoth to purchase tickets instead. It's also worth mentioning that at the games we can take MagicBands on iPod touches that only work half the time, so I usually don't even bother with them anymore.

Comet Crasher was the last game I was trained on, and, like Mammoth, working there can be a wonderful experience or a miserable one. At Comet, guests throw whiffle balls (err...I mean "comets") into the universe (a board with holes). If the "comet" lands in a "colored crater", they win a prize, and if it lands in a "black hole", they don't. It's a game of luck, not skill, and there is no way to be good at it. As a result, it can seem like a rip off, because guests can use a lot of balls and not win anything. However, the prizes at Comet are the largest of all the games, so if you win, you're winning something good.

I love Comet. It's cool to see how excited kids get when you give them a giant prize. And Comet is a game where if they lose, it's easy to just give them extra tries until they win, which makes both the kids and the parents happy. But I also hate Comet, because for whatever reason, I find that guests can become very demanding at this game, and that gets really old really fast. If a kid throws the ball and it doesn't make it to the holes, I always pick it up and give it back to them. What I don't like is when there are multiple kids playing, and

I'm already rushing around picking up balls, and parents are yelling at me saying things like:

"She dropped another one! It's right here...excuse me. Can you pick up this ball?! It's right over here on the ground. We need one more! Ours fell. The ball fell. It fell. On the ground. We need another ball. Pick it up. Pick up the ball for us! We need two more!"

Now that I've been working on the games for a while, I have mixed feelings. I usually don't want anything to do with the games. People are rude, kids cry, it's very repetitive, and I feel like a carny. While the games are much more physically (and sometimes emotionally) demanding than other Merchandise tasks, they can be rewarding as well. It's wonderful to give prizes to kids who didn't think they'd win anything and watch their faces light up. It's even more rewarding to go above and beyond for Make-A-Wish kids and their families, who are clearly going through a difficult time and could use the extra prizes.

There are also opportunities for Magical Moments. My favorite is when there is only one kid who wants to play a competition game, but there's no one around for her to play against. If this happens, we get another games Cast Member to play and really hype up that they're tough competition, and ultimately let the kid win. Doing this makes the kids feel special, like they were so good at the game they were even able to beat someone who works there.

It's the moments like that when I do really enjoy working on the games.

Chapter Twelve

You reach a point where you don't work for the money.

Walt Disney once said:

> Happiness is a state of mind. It's just according to the way you look at things. So I think happiness is contentment, but it doesn't mean you have to have wealth. All individuals are different and some of us just wouldn't be satisfied with just carrying out a routine job and being happy.

Working at Walt Disney World as a Cast Member is no "routine job" and it is certainly not something you do for the money. This is particularly true for CPs, who have rent taken out of their paychecks weekly and do not have bonuses or holiday pay. While the pay for this internship is very low, I do not think it is too low for what it entails. (Keep in mind that this is coming from someone who had two unpaid internships previous to this one. One of my previous internships I technically paid for myself, rather than got paid for the work. I needed to pay my college to earn credit for the internship, but the internship was not paid. So I essentially paid to participate in an internship. When you consider those scenarios, the Disney College Program pay seems like a six-figure salary.)

As a CP during my program, I made $9 an hour. After taxes and rent coming out of my paychecks, I averaged about $145 a week that actually went into my bank account. I know this sounds horrible, but it surprisingly wasn't. I did not bring a car to Florida, so the only expense that I needed weekly was food. And if you spend $145 on food for one person for a week, you're doing something wrong. I would usually go grocery shopping once every two or three weeks and spend about $100 each time. $100/2.5 weeks = $40 per week spent on groceries. Subtracting this money weekly from groceries would still leave me with at least $100. Without a car (to go anywhere besides Disney) and the fact that I could get into any Disney park for free whenever I wanted, it was easy to save money. That being said, it is tempting to go nuts spending money in Disney World, but if you have an ounce of self-control, you will be okay financially.

If you have a car, you would be saving less money per week because you'll be paying for gas. While the bus system is not ideal, I saved a lot of money by never having to fill up a gas tank. The bus system for CPs is (unfortunately) not run by Disney, but rather an outside company called Transtar. If you've been doing some research about the DCP, you've probably already heard some horror stories about Transtar, so allow me to debunk those for you. Contrary to what the internet may tell you, Transtar is extremely comparable, if not slightly better than most public bus systems. If I were to hop on an MBTA bus in Boston, I would likely find myself in close quarters with a whole host of characters who I would rather not have anywhere near my airspace. Similarly, the buses in Boston can take a long time to come, resulting in me standing outside in the middle of the city waiting. These are the prices you pay when you do not have a car and use public transportation, and the DCP buses are no different. (On the positive side, the Transtar buses are only for CPs living in Disney housing, so there are no random sketchy people on the bus with you like there would be in a city.) The people who complain about Transtar have either never taken public transportation before, or do not take it regularly enough to know that what they've experienced during the DCP is simply what happens when you do not have a car, and they would run into the same problems in any major city.

My biggest issue with the bus system is not Transtar's fault; it's the layout of Walt Disney World and Orlando that is to blame. For example, let's say I get out of work in Boston and need to pick up a couple of new outfits. I can leave work, walk for about 5 minutes, and hit a department store. What if that store is closed? A slightly longer walk in the opposite direction will bring me to a mall. Don't feel like walking to the mall? I can stop right where I am and wait for a bus that will take me there, or to a different mall.

Now let's say that I got out of work in Animal Kingdom and want to pick up a few outfits. My options of walking anywhere are gone, because there is absolutely nowhere within walking distance of the theme parks. After a 10-minute walk from my work location, I'll spend about 40 minutes waiting for a Transtar bus to arrive at the park to pick me up. Once I'm on the bus, I'll need to sit through stops at Animal Kingdom Lodge and ESPN Wide World of Sports, making my total bus ride another 35-40 minutes. I've now spent almost an hour and a half going from my work location to my apartment. Now that I'm back at Vista, I'll be waiting another 20 minutes for the Florida Mall bus, assuming it's one of the days that the bus actually goes there. (The bus only goes to the mall once or twice per week, usually not on my days off.) If it's not one of those days, I would just stay on the bus I got on at work and wait until it stops at the Commons, another DCP apartment complex. Then I could get off at the Commons and walk across the street and through a parking garage to the outlets.

So the problem with the Transtar buses is not that they take too long and break down sometimes (because that happens with every form of public transportation), but rather that Orlando is too spread out.

If it's financially feasible for you to bring a car, do it. You won't be dependent on the buses or on your roommates and friends to take you places, and you'll find that there's a lot to do outside the Disney bubble. Grocery shopping will be easy. Getting takeout will be easy. You'll have no problem visiting Universal. And, perhaps most important, some time away from Disney, by yourself, is often just what you'll need to put the magic back in your life.

Chapter Thirteen

Always, as you travel, assimilate the sounds and sights of the world.

One of my most cherished memories from my program was walking into the Magic Kingdom for the first time with our new company IDs. My roommates and I decided that as soon as we got our IDs, we would be going to the Magic Kingdom as our first park. The feeling of entering the Magic Kingdom for the first time as a Cast Member is a feeling to entering for the first time as a guest. The Festival of Fantasy parade, which I had not yet seen in person, was just finishing up when we entered, and the lyrics described our feelings perfectly:

> *Away we go, It's a festival of fantasy*
> *Beauty and majesty, shining magically*
> *Dreams that glow, wondrous dazzling brilliantly*
> *So away we go, it's a festival of fantasy*

Even though you'd expect us to be excited, this was no ordinary level of excitement. We were on an emotional high that is difficult to describe to someone who hasn't experienced it themselves. I would describe it as a mix of nostalgia, anxiousness, and honor. The nostalgia and anxiousness probably happiness to most people who walk through the gates of the Magic Kingdom, but in addition I felt truly honored to be working for this company.

There is no such thing as an average day during the Disney College Program. If I was not at work, I was in the parks as a guest. I went to the parks more than any other CP I knew. Throughout my entire program, I never lost the excitement of being able to go to a Disney park whenever I wanted. The only time I would not have gone to the parks were if I had called out of work (because getting caught using your main entrance pass or blue company ID on a day you called out sick is a terminable offense). If I had two days off per week, I spent at least one of those days in the parks. As my shifts often ended early (between 4:00 and 6:00 pm), I would sometimes bring a change of clothes to work with me and go to the parks immediately after my shift. There were times when I would get off work in DinoLand, change into regular clothes and throw my costume and black sneakers into a tote bag, and hop on the bus to the Magic Kingdom. Because Cast Members get free locker rentals, it was so easy to change and store my clothes in a locker at a different park. On my days off, I usually went to the parks with friends, but after work I'd go alone.

Visiting the parks alone is not nearly as bad as it sounds; in fact, I don't mind going alone at all. I would especially enjoy going to the parks alone if I went after work and did not have much time. Being by myself would allow me to go to Magic Kingdom, get some corndog nuggets from Casey's Corner, ride Space Mountain, and go home, without worrying about what anyone else wanted to do in the park.

Solo trips to the park have also allowed me to meet guests from around the world, in a way that simply could not have happened during a shift at my work location. One such experience took place at one of my favorite restaurants: you guessed it, Casey's Corner. When you visit the parks regularly by yourself, eating out alone is not a horrifying concept like you'd imagine it to be. The only really terrible part about eating alone at a quick service restaurant is that finding a table on a crowded day, or during a lunch rush, can be difficult by yourself. Many families have someone save seats at a table while someone else waits in line for food, but I can't do that if I'm by myself. On this particular day, after I got my corn dog nuggets and drink, I walked over to the outdoor seating area and managed to find one empty table. I immediately swiped it, almost feeling guilty that here I was alone, during the lunch rush, at a table with three empty chairs. After a few minutes, a woman who appeared to be about my age approached my table. I assumed she was going to ask if she could take one of the empty chairs away, but instead she asked if she could sit with me. At first I thought this was an odd question, as people generally just ask if they can take the chair, not if they can share the table. But I was by myself, and most of the table was empty, so I told her that she was more than welcome to sit there.

We began talking, and she told me about how she was traveling up and down the East Coast with two of her roommates from her university, who later joined us at the table. They were all from Singapore, and had never been to the United States before. At one point they asked me if I was local to the parks, so I told them about how I was on a college internship working Merchandise in Animal Kingdom. They were thrilled to be eating lunch with a Disney Cast Member. We spent some time discussing their plans for the rest of the day and I gave them some restaurant recommendations. (They needed a nice dinner later to make up for their experience at Casey's. The three ordered chili cheese dogs, and "chili" in Singapore is not the same as "chili" in the U.S., so needless to say their meals were not what they expected.) I sat at the table for about 15 minutes after I had finished my nuggets to continue the conversation we'd been having.

A few weeks later, I was in the Magic Kingdom by myself again, eating lunch at an empty table at Pecos Bill's. While I was about halfway through my meal, a middle-aged woman approached the table and asked if she could sit down. She had a very heavy German accent, and she already had her tray of food, which led me to believe that she was also eating alone. I asked her if her family or friends would be joining us, and she told me that she was indeed from Germany and that she was visiting Walt Disney World alone. She had made it a life goal to visit each Disney park around the world at least once, and the U.S. parks were the only ones she had left. Immediately after her last day at Disney World, she would be heading to Disneyland before going home to Germany.

Experiences like these were my favorite parts of visiting the parks alone. If I had met these people while I was working, there would have been little opportunity to get to know them. Before I began my program, I would have never thought that I'd have impromptu lunch dates with people from Singapore and Germany. I also found it interesting that every time I was in a restaurant solo, and someone approached me about sharing the table, the someone was never American. Time and time again I saw guests, who I assume were from this country, look at my empty table and either walk away or stand around and wait for someone to leave.

You often hear that Americans have a different concept of personal space compared to people from other cultures. Perhaps we're the ones in the wrong here. A table for four can comfortably fit four people, whether you know them personally or not. I'll admit that during that first meal with the girls from Singapore at Casey's, I was slightly uncomfortable at the thought of sharing a table at Disney World with strangers, but looking back on it I am so happy I did. Being at the world's most visited tourist destination for an extended period of time allows you to learn a lot about different cultures and customs around the world, and I would not have had some of these experiences if a total stranger had not asked me if she could sit at my table.

Another memorable experience took place during my first visit to Epcot during the DCP. My roommate Holly and I went to Epcot one night just to get margaritas from Mexico and watch Illuminations. Because we arrived so late, we decided that it was not worth it to fight for a spot near the water to see the fireworks, so we headed toward the benches between Mexico and Future World. There, we met two women from the U.K. who were visiting Disney World for the first time. When the fireworks started, one of the women stood up from the bench to see better, and began oohing and aahing. Her friend, who was not interested in standing up from the bench, told us that Illuminations was what she was most looking forward to during their whole trip. The expression on this woman's face while she watched Illuminations for the first time reminded me again how special my experience of working for Disney would be. This grown woman had been looking forward to seeing Illuminations for years, and the expression on her face demonstrated her emotions perfectly.

That Disney has the ability to bring ear-to-ear smiles and tears of joy to a grown woman during a 12-minute fireworks display is just one of the many reasons why working here is an incredible experience. I can't think of any other company that brings such magic to its customers.

Of course, some of my favorite memories as a guest took place while my family and friends from home were visiting. I completed the Tower of Terror 10 Miler, attended Mickey's Not So Scary and Very Merry Christmas Parties with friends from home. I spent a night in Downtown Disney (that was well worth calling out of work for) with some friends I hadn't seen in a couple of years. I spent a week with my parents and grandparents as well, both of whom came to visit more than once during my program. But my most memorable experience occurred when Chaz came to visit in September.

Before I left for the DCP, I did not think that being away from Chaz would be nearly as difficult as it was. I had lived away at school for most of the time that we had been together, and so I was not too concerned about an even greater distance between us. By the time

I had arrived in Orlando for the DCP, we were pros at going long periods of time without seeing each other. I thought everything would be fine—slightly inconvenient, but fine. I was wrong. It was not difficult because of the distance, or because of how long we would be apart—it was difficult because we had both applied to the program and only one of us had made it. There were times when I would tell him about my day and feel guilty that he wasn't there to experience it with me. When Chaz came to visit in September, applications had just gone live for the Spring 2015 program. He had submitted his application a few days before arriving in Orlando, which resulted in us compulsively checking his application status for updates all week.

During the second day of his visit, we visited Epcot and had an amazing lunch at Le Cellier. After lunch, we planned on heading out of the park to spend the rest of the night at Magic Kingdom. On our way out, we stopped behind Spaceship Earth to take a photo with one of the PhotoPass photographers stationed there. Just when I and the photographer thought we were done taking pictures, Chaz asked if we could take one more, and he pulled a small box out of his bag. The photographer picked up on what was happening and began snapping away as Chaz got down on one knee and asked me to marry him. By the time he had gotten all of the words out, and I had said yes, a small crowd formed behind the photographer and began cheering for us. At this point we were both crying, and I remember not even being able to see the ring clearly for about another 10 minutes because of the tears in my eyes. My ring, by the way, which Chaz picked out by himself, is designed to look like the sun from the banners in *Tangled*, my favorite Disney movie. We immediately set off to Guest Relations to get our Just Engaged buttons, and our next stop was a ride on Spaceship Earth.

When I tell people that I got engaged at Disney World, they usually expect it to have taken place in front of Cinderella Castle. But the castle is not my favorite place in Disney—Spaceship Earth is. Spaceship Earth has always been my favorite attraction, and the ride has even more meaning for me now as a writer and a history major. The concept of the ride encompasses so many of my interests, and I think its design and history are fascinating, too. I'm ecstatic to have gotten engaged near Spaceship Earth, because now my favorite part of Disney will always be special for the two of us.

Nothing will ever top that last experience, but there are plenty of other amazing memories I have from my program as a guest:

- Meeting Richard, the greeter outside the Grand Floridian, on multiple occasions, and him telling me that I look as grand as the resort.
- Visiting the parks with fellow CPs who had never been to them before.
- Eating and drinking around the world with my friends during the Food and Wine Festival.
- Finishing my first 10-mile race and meeting four Disney characters along the way.
- Riding Tower of Terror for the first time ever. (Sorry, Joshua! I hope your arm and ears have recovered!)
- Riding Space Mountain with the lights on. (Now that I think of it, this one might actually be one of my worst memories as a guest.)

Chapter Fourteen

In order to make good in your chosen task, it's important to have someone you want to do it for. The greatest moments in life are not concerned with selfish achievements but rather for the things we do for the people we love and esteem, and whose respect we need.

Because this is the college program after all, and I did come here to work, I suppose I should tell you about some of my most memorable experiences while on the clock.

While I did not enjoy working the carnival games in Dino-Rama, they did have their moments. There is no other feeling in the world that can compare to seeing the smile on a child's face when they win a prize at one of the Fossil Fun Games. And being the person who gives them the prize is an incredible experience. The same goes for their parents. There was one day where two twin girls were playing Mammoth Marathon, a competition game—meaning only one of them would win. I could see the anxiety on their parents' faces while they watched the girls play, probably trying to figure out how they were going to handle it when only one of them got a prize.

"And it looks like we have a tie! Congratulations, you both did awesome!"

Problem solved.

Were we supposed to give out extra prizes left and right? No. This was an instance where we were told to use our discretion. Using your discretion is something you're told about a lot in training, so I guess management just trusts that we know what kind of discretion to have and it wouldn't vary from person to person. I'm pretty sure every Cast Member in DinoLand gives out more games prizes than management would like, but they're "using their discretion", right?

Another nice thing about the games was that I was in complete control. I could say whatever I wanted (within reason, of course) the microphone, and do whatever I wanted with the game. If I wanted to play a kids only game with no adults, I could do that because I was in control. I could do things like let kids "practice" for free, because their parents were not interested in paying for tickets. If a parent made it clear that they were not buying games tickets, but the child still wanted to play, I'd give him a ball or turn the game on and say, "Without a ticket you can still practice!" I'd stop after a few minutes, tell them they did great, and usually notice very happy parents whose child was no longer tormenting them about playing the games.

One of the most rewarding experiences I've had at work, that is much more specific to Disney than other companies, is working with Make-A-Wish kids and their parents. It is one of the most rewarding, and one of the most difficult, things I have ever done. You can visibly see everything these families are going through just by the looks on the parents' faces, which makes you want to do everything in your power to make their trip to Disney World extra special. If I was working one of the non-competition style games in DinoLand, the Make-A-Wish kids always won. If a Make-A-Wish kid didn't succeed with any of his four shots on Comet Crasher, I'd put four more balls in front of him without taking another ticket. And when he did win, I'd give him one of the bigger prizes regardless of where the ball actually landed.

One of the most touching experiences with a Make-A-Wish family occurred when I was at the photo counter in the Dino Institute. When Make-A-Wish families come to Disney World, they get a special PhotoPass card with the Genie on it so they can download their ride photos for free. They would still have to pay for prints, but they can download whichever photos they'd like without paying anything extra. The family consisted of a little boy and his parents, all three of them wearing blue Make-A-Wish buttons. The little boy, who was about 6 or 7 years old, told me about how he collects buttons, but the only button he had at the moment was the one he was wearing—the blue Make-A-Wish button.

"Is it your first time here?" I asked him.

"Mhmm."

"Oh! Well, then, you need a first visit button!" I grabbed a first visit button out of a cabinet behind the register and gave it to him.

One of my coworkers took a birthday button out of the drawer and told him that you can celebrate your birthday year round at Disney World.

"I think you need a celebration button to go with that birthday button!"

And before you knew it, he was wearing four buttons, his Make-A-Wish button at the highest point of his shirt, above birthday, celebration, and first visit buttons.

"Now I have four buttons!" The little boy was so excited that much of his t shirt was now covered in the different buttons.

As I was putting their photo into a folder, *of course I printed it for free, shhhh*, the boy's father looked at me and said:

"I'd give anything in the world for him to not have that top button."

I didn't know how to respond. Becoming emotional while you're working is unprofessional, and looking extremely sad to a Make-A-Wish family probably wouldn't help the situation. I think the parents realized that I didn't quite know how else to respond, so the boy's mother thanked me profusely for all of the buttons to slightly change the subject. I smiled and handed them their free 8x10 and went to the backroom of the photo area for some tissues.

Most of the time when you work with Make-A-Wish kids at Disney, you aren't with them long enough, nor do the correct conversations arise, for you to fully process their situation. When a Make-A-Wish kid plays one of the carnival games, he or she is focused on the game, and the foundation is never mentioned—I just notice it from the buttons or t shirts. The first time the Make-A-Wish Foundation became a part of actual conversation with a guest was that day at the Dino Institute, and keeping my emotions in check was probably one of the hardest things I've ever had to do at work. While working with Make-A-Wish kids and their families is not easy, it's extremely rewarding. That little boy's day was made, in part because I added to his button collection, and that is one work experience that I will never forget.

One of the best parts about working in Merchandise is that you can pick up shifts in almost any other Merchandise location on Disney property. During my program, I was able to work at DinoLand, Frontierland, Tomorrowland, Future World, the Land, the Grand Floridian, and Mickey's Not so Scary Halloween Party.

My favorite place to pick up shifts was Gateway Gifts/Camera Center in Future World. These shops are the two right in the front of the park, directly to either side of Spaceship Earth. I enjoyed being near the park entrance and seeing the excitement on guests' faces as they walked into Epcot. I also, of course, loved being near Spaceship Earth, which worked out perfectly because guests would ask me about the ride all the time. I've done quite a bit of research on Spaceship Earth and have ridden it numerous times in a row, so I guess you could say I'm a bit of an expert on that attraction. Lexie has told me that I probably know more about it than the Cast Members who work there. The location also had some variety in the things you would do there for Merchandise. Gateway Gifts has a model of Spaceship Earth that opens up to be a pin holder so guests can trade pins from it. And Camera Center is where you get locker rentals and can look up Leave a Legacy photos. And I love the costume—it's a purple shirt with Spaceship Earth all over it.

Frontierland was my second favorite place to pick up shifts. I loved the costume—a powder blue pioneer-era dress—and I also loved the ways you could merchantain with the products sold there. At Big Al's, the cart across from the Country Bear Jamboree, I learned how to correctly hold the different kinds of toy guns for when kids asked how to use them. There's something really cool about wearing a pretty dress while showing off my newfound rifle skills. My favorite time to work at Big Al's was during parades. I worked in Frontierland twice during a Halloween party night at the Magic Kingdom, and during the pre-show for the parade, I was able to wear the glow merchandise and participate in the mini-dance party.

Speaking of Halloween party nights, one of my favorite shifts ever was a treat shift that I miraculously was able to pick up. Anyone can work the shifts to give out Halloween candy, but Cast Members who actually work in those locations are scheduled for them, so it makes it more difficult for non-Magic Kingdom Cast Members to get these shifts. I was able to pick up a shift for the Adventureland Treat Trail, where I was placed by the exit of Pirates of the Caribbean. Treat shifts are the best: you get to wear the Halloween party costume (which is one of my favorites) and you get paid to give out candy. And, since you are always being rotated or going on break, the shift goes by really fast. At Pirates, we had 1 entry greeter, 2 candy givers, and 1 exit greeter. But there were 5 Cast Members working there, so someone was always on break. Every 15 minutes we would rotate and someone else would go on. I was only able to pick up one of these shifts during my program, but I'm so happy I did.

Chapter Fifteen

*When they come here, they're coming because of an
integrity that we've established over the years. And they drive
hundreds of miles. I feel a responsibility to the public.*

Unfortunately, like any other job, working for Disney is not 100%
magic, 100% of the time. If you're looking for a major tell-all about the
company, you've picked up the wrong book, but I will tell you some of
the things that were a little less than magical for me, beginning with:

Games. I've said it before, I'll say it again: I didn't like working
the games. I didn't hate it, because there were some good moments,
but on the whole, I disliked almost everything about working the
games. Most of the issues I have with games are similar to PAC, or
Parade Audience Control. (I should also mention that if you're reading
this, and you're a future DinoLand or PAC CP, please don't take
everything I have to say to heart. There are some CPs who absolutely
love these roles; I just was not one of them.) I really disliked the
ways that guests treat you when you're working the games. Now,
you can get crazy or rude guests everywhere, in any line of business,
but there was definitely a higher concentration of them in games
compared to other places I've worked. (I would say that PAC is similar,
because you basically tell people that they can't stand where they're
standing for the parade, and some of those guests don't want to
hear it, and will you so.) At the games, one of my biggest issues was
non-playing guests clamoring for attention while I was trying to
spiel for playing guests.

"Once we get started those dinos are going to pop out of the holes
in front of you. You just want to wha—"

"HOW MUCH ARE TICKETS?!"

"whack them really ha—"

"WHERE DO I BUY TICKETS!?!? HOW MUCH ARE THEY!?!?"

"You can get tickets right at the pin cart behind you *two finger
Disney point*. They are 1 for $4, 3 for $10, or 5 for $15, and you need

1 ticket per person per game. So anyway, you need to whack those dinos on the hea—"

"WHERE DO YOU GET THEM? WHAT CART?! I DON'T SEE A CART!"

"The one right over here *two finger Disney point again* with all of the pins on the side and the red roof and the sign that says 'Shop Til You're Dizzy' located directly behind you and in front of Triceratop Spin, just about 4 feet away from where you're currently standing..." *Oh, you're walking away. Now where was I...*

"Alright, sorry about that, just whack them on the head, the first player to 150 is our winner! And go! Oh, and don't use your hands, those dinosaurs are hungry, only use—"

"HEY! CAN I GET TICKETS HERE?"

Anytime you have a job where you work with the public, you can expect to get interrupted, because so many people have entitlement issues and don't care that there are others already being helped. On games, however, I found this to be stressful while I was trying to spiel. It's also different than being interrupted at a cash register. I can finish a transaction while answering someone else's question, but it's physically impossible for me to tell a group of guests how to play a game and answer some random question at the same time, especially when I was new to spieling and found it difficult to get back into the swing of it once I'd been interrupted.

Guests at the games also become very demanding in a way that didn't happen as much at regular merchandise locations. They'd want prizes even though they lost, they'd want to play again for free, they'd want different color prizes, or different sizes that they didn't win, they'd want to play by themselves so they'd definitely win. If all of these were phrased in the form of questions rather than orders, it wouldn't have been bad, but often guests would throw orders at me. Maybe it was the carnival atmosphere of Chester and Hester's that made them forget they were in the magical, happy world of Disney.

Working games also means that you're most likely outside all day. When you sign up to work for Disney, you are told that you could be put outside all day, so it shouldn't come as much of a surprise. Even with the advance warning, however, Florida heat and humidity is a shocker. I stopped wearing makeup to my DinoLand shifts because it was so hot inside the games that my mascara would melt. The heat wasn't bad if I was placed at a cart, since then you're not moving around (aka working up a sweat). But in the games you're constantly walking back and forth, reaching up high, bending down, or in the case of Comet Crasher, literally crawling on the ground (to pick up dropped whiffle balls, I mean comets). On the plus side, DinoLand was on top of making sure we were always okay outside. Someone would always have the task of filling up water bottles for outdoor Cast Members so you would never be without cold water, and there was shade and/or fans everywhere. You do get used to the heat and being outside all day, but it still is not an ideal situation.

If you're sensitive to what goes on backstage in Disney World, you might want to skip this part, as it is NSFM (Not Safe for Magic). Some of my worst memories from working in Disney were seeing characters backstage. Disney upholds and promotes the basic premise that all characters are real, and there is only one of each of them. While character integrity is important to create a magical environment for guests onstage, everyone who works at Disney knows someone who is "friends with" a character, and will likely see them out of costume at some point during their career. Seeing characters out of costume is not something I enjoyed on my college program.

Here comes the NSFM...

It was my first day working in DinoLand without a trainer. Overall, the day went well, and I was excited to go home and relax. After my shift, I went through the backstage gate near DINOSAUR, which leads to a road (behind Restaurantosaurus) that goes back to the entrance of the park. As I passed the Restaurantosaurus break rooms, Pluto and his character attendant walked past me, also coming from onstage.

That's kind of cool. I can see characters back here even when I'm not in the park. Wait, what's he doing?...

Pluto reached his right arm behind his back near the collar of the costume and with one quick pull, ZIP! (or UNZIP!, I guess I should say.)

NSFM! Why is this happening!?

Pluto was now Pluto only from the waist down, and a very sweaty human from the waist up. (My first week was in August, remember, so the heat and humidity were in full swing.) I stopped in my path, my jaw dropped, and I just stared. I'm pretty sure I was on the verge of tears. Now I'm not an idiot, I know there are people inside the costumes. I just think that Disney does such a good job with promoting character integrity and designing the costumes that it's never so obvious. I've been to other amusement parks where you see characters and immediately think, "Oh, that's just a person." But Disney was never like that for me. I knew there were people in there, because logically there had to be, but it was so far out of sight that it truly was out of mind.

While Pluto was still walking to the entertainment trailer, Goofy and his character attendant walked by me going toward the gate to go onstage.

"Hi, there!" I looked over to the character attendant, still trying to keep some sense of composure.

"Say hi to Goofy!"

Goofy waved at me, and I waved back. He pointed at my shorts, and then pointed at his shorts. (When Goofy meets guests in DinoLand, he wears the same tacky dinosaur shorts the Cast Members in Dino-Rama wear.) I laughed at his silent mention of our matching outfits, and finally started walking again toward the park entrance.

That character attendant must have noticed that I was shaken up from seeing half-dressed Pluto, and so she tried to distract me with fully-dressed Goofy. Her distraction worked, and I'm thankful for that, because otherwise I probably would have spent another 10 minutes standing there trying to forget what I just saw. As my program went on, I still didn't like seeing characters out of costume, but I was able to get over it. It was the first time that was extremely shocking and uncomfortable.

For whatever reason, seeing face characters out of costume was not nearly as scarring for me. I think it might be because I didn't see a face character out of costume until a about a month into my program when I picked up a shift in Tomorrowland. I left to go to my shift early, because I needed to pick up the costume first and I didn't want to get lost in the Utilidors. I found where I needed to go quicker than I thought I would have, so I had about an hour left before my shift started. I decided to go to the Mouseketeria, the cast cafeteria located in the tunnel.

I found my way to the Mouse and got in line at Subway...behind Ariel. Or rather, behind someone who was friends with Ariel, I should say. Her hair and makeup were done as Ariel, but she was wearing a t shirt and sweatpants, looking at her iPhone, and ordering a sandwich from Subway. I'm not going to lie, I did stare. It's not something you see every day, but it was not nearly as traumatizing as the fur characters. I was able to get over this much quicker than the Pluto incident, or at least I had to, because a friend of Wendy from *Peter Pan* joined me at my lunch table that day.

Speaking of Tomorrowland, one of my worst work experiences happened during that same shift. Tomorrowland was the first non-DinoLand shift I had, so I was still inexperienced at picking up shifts in different areas and I wasn't quite sure how it all worked. I had been told that I would be able to clock in and get assignments on their computers, but that I wouldn't be able to log into their register system unless a manager added me to it.

I arrived at Tomorrowland and immediately clocked in and found a manager. I told her that I was EHH (Extra Hours Hotline—basically that I didn't work there regularly and only had that shift for the day) and that she would need to add me to the system. She told me I was all set. That seemed weird to me, because I was almost positive that I was going to have to do something to get onto the register, but she seemed fine with it, so I trusted her.

At the morning meeting, the manager told us that it would only be "kind of busy, at an expected attendance of 57,000". To put this into perspective, Animal Kingdom management is happy if we hit 25,000, so I was little worried that Magic Kingdom would be a lot to handle coming from DinoLand. Once the meeting was over, we lined up at the computer to pick up our assignments.

My assignment slip read: "Brittany, please pick up position: URSA CART." *Ursa Cart? What's that?*

I checked with the manager, who informed me that it was the hat cart outside of Space Mountain and reassured me that I was all set to go and open the cart. When I got to the cart, there were already guests running toward Space Mountain, even though the park had only been open for about 2 minutes. Ursa Cart was not like any cart we had in DinoLand. DinoLand carts were one single cart, whereas this cart had 2 separate sections: a glow station and a drink area. Once I got the cart open, I went to log on to the register. As I half-expected, my login information didn't work.

Alright...where is the phone, I'll just figure out who to call and... Is that the phone?

I looked behind the register and found a black Motorola walkie talkie. I had never used a walkie, so I wasn't quite sure what to do.

While I was examining the walkie, a guest came up to the register to buy something. So now I was at a cart, alone, in a park that on any given day has more than 4 times the number of guests that my park had, with a register I couldn't log on to, and a guest waiting to check out.

Well, I know the basics of using a walkie is that you hold down the button and talk. It must be this big one on the side.

Beep "Hi, this is Brittany, I'm at the Ursa Cart, and I can't log in to the register...over."

I'm not sure if you're actually supposed to say "over", but they always say it in movies and it sounded right at the time.

I explained to the guest that I didn't usually work in Tomorrowland, and that I was sorry about the delay, but the register was giving me a hard time. Thankfully, her husband and son planned on riding Space Mountain, and she had nothing else to do but wait.

I guess I should try the walkie again. It probably doesn't look good to guests if I'm just standing here not doing anything to fix the situation.

Beep "It's Brittany again, at Ursa, I still can't get into the register...it says my password is invalid. It's probably because I'm EHH. So if someone could get down here to the cart, I could—" I saw a Tomorrowland coordinator approaching the cart. "Never mind, over and out."

"I'll stay here, you head back to the manager's office and tell them you need to be put in the system," he said when he reached the cart.

"Okay, thank you."

"Oh, and by the way, there's a menu button on the walkie. You press menu, then contacts, then MOD. You just sent that message to everyone in the park who has a walkie."

That's embarrassing. How many people can say they accidentally paged an entire theme park's employee base? I hope I was correct using the word "over", otherwise I'll have sounded extra stupid.

After I met with the manager again, I was all set to go on the register and the rest of my shift went smoothly. She just heard me incorrectly in the morning and thought I'd be all set. I guess I'm not sure if that was one of my *worst* moments at work, but it was definitely one of the more embarrassing ones. I'm sure there was some Cast Member listening to my call for help working somewhere like Adventureland and wondering why he should care about poor Brittany at the Ursa Cart.

Another embarrassing moment also took place when I worked in Magic Kingdom, on the night of my treat shift for the Halloween party. I had heard from other DinoLand CPs who picked up shifts in other areas that it can be really confusing to get around when it's somewhere you've never been before, so I left about 3 hours early for my shift in case I got horribly lost. Ordinarily, when you pick up shifts in different areas, the form you receive tells you where to meet.

For Merchandise, it's pretty easy to figure out even if you don't know where you're going, because you at least know where the stores are from onstage. When I worked in Epcot for the first time, I wasn't sure how to get to the stock room of Gateway Gifts, so I just walked into the store from onstage and asked the Cast Members working there. The Magic Kingdom is different. The Utilidor was specifically created so that guests wouldn't see Cast Members in different costumes in parts of the park where they don't belong. (Walt Disney once saw a cowboy walk through Tomorrowland in Disneyland, and believed that it took away from the area's detailed theming.) The strict rules for how far you can go in a particular costume makes it difficult to walk onstage in the Magic Kingdom when you're trying to find your work location.

Anyway, the form I received told me to meet at the Attractions manager's office in Adventureland. I walked through the tunnel and found my way toward Adventureland, but saw no sign of the manager's office. *Is it even in the tunnel? How am I supposed to find this place?*

Judging by the map on the wall, I decided to take one of the Adventureland/Frontierland elevators up to see if the office was on another floor. One floor up on the elevator brought me to a narrow, off white hallway.

This doesn't seem right. But then again, I have no idea what I'm even looking for...

I opened one door a crack and peeked through. I saw that it led to the Trading Post in Frontierland, so that would be incorrect. I went back down the hallway to another door, peeked through, and saw the money room for the Trading Post.

Where is Adventureland? The sign downstairs said Adventureland/ Frontierland, but this is only Frontierland. Adventureland should be behind all this, on the other side of the Trading Post building...

I hopped back into the elevator, and noticed a "3" button, meaning that there was a third floor. *If I just came out into the Trading Post, how can there even be a third floor? Unless it goes up to the second floor of the Trading Post's building...*

I pushed the button and left the elevator through a door oppo-site the one I entered through. *Now that makes sense, because Adventureland is behind me. But is Adventureland really another floor up from Frontierland?*

When I exited the elevator through the back, there was a computer. I tried to clock in on it, but it didn't let me, meaning I was still in the wrong place. There were three doors leading from this small room. I could see that one led to a stock room for what looked like Pirates of the Caribbean merchandise, but I couldn't tell where the other two doors went, and of course they were windowless and unlabeled. When an Adventureland Cast Member came in to use the computer, I asked him for directions.

"Out that door and to the right," he said.

That doesn't sound difficult, the office must be right there.

I pushed open the door and found myself onstage, in Adventureland, in my Halloween party costume, when the party didn't start for another three hours, in the only park that is insanely strict about where you wear your costumes. Immediately, one of the Adventureland Merchandise managers noticed my state of confusion and walked me over to the Attractions managers office, which happened to be in a trailer behind the Tiki Room. If you ever can't find something in Disney, it's probably in a trailer, which makes it easy to miss if that's not what you see in your head when you think of an office.

But as I mentioned before, this was one of my favorite nights to work. The shift was so much fun, but getting there was a bit difficult if you're not used to the tunnel. It's not Disney's fault. The walls in the tunnels are color coded and there are maps everywhere. And if you ask others they are always willing to help; it's just that backstage at Disney looks so different from backrooms at any other job that you can't just logically figure out where you're going. (I also don't understand that elevator. Floor 1—tunnel. Floor 2—Trading Post. Floor 3—Adventureland. How does that even make sense? How does one floor come out into a gift shop in Frontierland, and the floor above it is Adventureland? Adventureland doesn't seem like it's a floor above Frontierland, so how do they do that? Must be magic.)

Chapter Sixteen

Childishness? I think it's the equivalent of never losing your sense of humor. I mean, there's a certain something that you retain. It's the equivalent of not getting so stuffy that you can't laugh at others.

One of the perks of participating in the Disney College Program is being able to take classes for free. The program offers collegiate level classes, as well as seminar-style classes. I opted to take one of the seminar classes, as I had already graduated from college and did not need the credit. The seminar was perfect. As long as you showed up you received a certificate of completion, and there was no mandatory homework or assignments like in ordinary college classes. It was very laid back and met every Friday morning for eight weeks.

The class I took was Exploring Marketing, part of the Disney Exploration Series of seminars that focus on different aspects of the Walt Disney Company. It was the most interesting "business" class I have ever taken. Our facilitator, an alum of the college program, used the marketing plans for New Fantasyland to tie together all of the concepts we learned in the class. In addition, each week we had guest speakers who worked in marketing in different areas throughout the company. On the last day of class, they all returned for a question-and-answer session. While it was sometimes difficult to get up for a class at 8:00 am on Friday mornings, especially if I had working late the night before, the class was well worth taking.

Other perks of working for Disney are primarily in the form of discounts. The money I've saved through Disney discounts is unbelievable. I remember working at Staples and being excited when they finally gave us a 10% discount, which is nothing compared to what Disney offers. I got up to 60% off hotel rooms, 20-40% off merchandise, 20-40% off dining, a variety of discounts on Disney recreational offerings, 20% off quick service meals at Animal Kingdom and the resorts, and a holiday coupon book which included 30%, 40%, and

50% off meal coupons, free popcorn and soda coupons, free PhotoPass downloads, free rounds of mini golf, and extra park tickets.

Of course, the biggest perk is free park admission. Even toward the end of my program, it was a weird feeling seeing other guests in line to spend hundreds of dollars on tickets while I walk into the park for free. The best part was the ability to leisurely walk around and not have to rush to attractions and shows. If I ever missed something I wanted to see or do, it was no big deal, because I could come back the next day, or the day after that, or the day after that. It wasn't like being on vacation, where if you don't squeeze everything you want to do into a week you may never have the chance to do it again.

Cast Members can also sign up for tickets to attend the Christmas day parade filming. I did it once, just to see what it would be like. On the appointed day, I arrived at the Magic Kingdom at 5:00 am and waited until about 6:00 am, when we were herded onto Main Street. Once there, a group of us was taken to Liberty Square to be included in the filming for one of the *Star Wars* scenes. I was eventually moved to the riverboat, which they filmed in the background of the opening scene for the parade. While it was really cool to see how the parade is filmed, it was also exhausting: they did multiple takes and they want you to be cheering, clapping, or waving the entire time.

As for seeing myself on TV? I think I've successfully identified which dot on the deck of the riverboat I am, though it's still up for debate. It seems like they didn't use the footage of me in Liberty Square, but it was a memorable experience nonetheless.

Another perk is backstage tours of attractions and shows. Many work locations set up behind-the-scenes tours for the Cast Members stationed there. I've been on two of them with my DinoLand co-workers: The Great Movie Ride and Lights, Motors, Action! The Movie Ride tour was everything I expected it to be, and more. We learned a lot of backstage info about the ride and its design, and we were able to get up close to many of the sets to take photos. The Lights, Motors, Action! tour exceeded my expectations, which were not set very high. While I've always appreciated the hard work that goes into performing this show, it has never been one of my favorites. It's one of those performances that I see once and I won't feel the need to see again for a long time. The backstage tour, however, was very interesting, and it made me want to see the show more. It didn't hurt that we had the chance to sit inside the stunt cars for photos.

Chapter Seventeen

Never get bored or cynical. Yesterday is a thing of the past.

As my program drew to an end, it was time to prepare myself for a number of changes coming my way. Two of my roommates, Holly and Lexie, moved out of our apartment in mid-December. Holly extended her CP into a role in housekeeping for the spring, and Lexie applied for part-time work with Disney. With Holly and Lexie gone, our apartment felt empty and much less homey than it did before. Paulina and I had such opposite schedules, with me working in Animal Kingdom and her working in Magic Kingdom, that we almost never saw one another in the apartment. On the plus side, Paulina and I each got to have our own bedrooms and bathrooms for a couple of weeks, and I even pushed the two twin beds together in my room. There are no hard feelings about them leaving; it just became sort of weird to almost always be alone in an apartment that used to have four girls living there. Technically, the housing committee could have put more roommates in our apartment, but they never did, so Paulina and I were the only ones who finished the program in our apartment at Vista Way.

The last couple of weeks of the college program are filled with a number of farewell-style events. I applied, and was accepted, to extend my CP, but I was waiting for Chaz to hear back about his application before I committed to stay in Florida. After what felt like years of waiting to hear back, we learned that Chaz was accepted into the Disney College Program 2015 season. For the Spring program, I will be working in Attractions at Hollywood Studios, and Chaz will be working in Custodial on Main Street. Had Chaz not been accepted, I don't think I would have accepted my offer to stay. I love working for Disney, don't get me wrong, but I want to start working on my master's degree and find a job at home. Now, however, after being long distance for so much of our relationship, and being recently engaged, I have no desire to go back home if Chaz will be in Florida.

I'm excited for my new role in Attractions and to experience what it's like to work in Hollywood Studios.

Our CP graduation took place in early December, before the busy holiday season hit. The CP graduation was not a ceremony, like a typical college graduation, but rather a leisurely get-together that took place at one of the apartment complexes. We were able to drop by whenever we wanted for catered food, dancing, and photo opportunities in photo booths as well as with some of the characters in graduation attire. And, of course, we were able to pick up our certificate of completion and graduation ear hats. Holly and I attended the graduation together, though it did not feel like the end for us. It felt like the halfway mark, because it was. We were now staying in Florida until at least May, so our Fall 2014 graduation did not seem as monumental as it should have. After our graduation, Holly and I spent the night in Epcot, wandering through World Showcase. We also stopped by Mouse Gear to get our ear hats embroidered. Instead of the usual "DCP 2014" that it seems like everyone has done, we wanted to make our hats specific to where we worked—Skipper Holly and Cousin Britt.

The only other big CP send-off event left was a formal themed as the Courtyard of Good and Evil and held at the convention center at Coronado Springs. I went to it with Lexie, who agreed that all we really cared about was the free food and meeting characters. The event itself was very well done, though we had our priorities set on meeting rare characters rather than dancing. It was also the first dance I had been to without Chaz since I was a junior in high school; going without a date felt a little strange to me. Lexie and I had a great time, though. We got to meet some of our favorite characters, including Hades, Maleficent, and the Magic Mirror.

Epilogue

Why worry? If you've done the very best you can,
worrying won't make it any better. I worry about many
things, but not about water over the dam.

Now that you've heard about my experiences in the Fall 2014 Disney College Program, you're probably wondering what's next. My immediate future includes a new adventure on the Spring 2015 College Program, after which I'll finally return home to Massachusetts.

What's next from there? I don't know. I guess what you really want to know is whether or not I'll be applying for any other positions with Disney. No, I won't.

Let's rewind a bit. About halfway through my Fall 2014 program, I applied for some Professional Internships. These internships are essentially the next step above the college program if you plan to work your way up in the company. I applied for all of the education-based internships that would have involved working with the cultural representatives at the Animal Kingdom Lodge, and for the coveted role of Guest Relations intern within any of the parks. For as long as I can remember, it's been a dream of mine to work in Guest Relations at Walt Disney World, particularly in the Magic Kingdom. It was a dream similar to my ambitions regarding the program. I wanted to do it, but it just seemed so much like it wasn't going to happen that I kind of pushed the thought aside and forgot about it. But when applications for the Guest Relations internship came out, I jumped at the opportunity and submitted a resume and cover letter right away.

I had three interviews for the internships, all of which I felt went only okay—they weren't horrible, but they weren't my best, either. For weeks, I waited for a decision, and yet week after week, I heard nothing. Then I noticed on Facebook that other applicants were receiving offers. I was realistic, and did not allow this news to get my hopes up.

Then one day, while I was on my break in DinoLand, I checked my email on my phone. Inside my inbox were 3 rejection emails for the internships I had applied for. My reaction, perhaps surprisingly, was more confusion than sadness. I had just been rejected for my dream job, and I will never have a chance to apply for it again. How am I doing so well? I was not heartbroken. I was doing just fine. And that was the moment I realized that staying in Orlando and working for Disney was not the right decision for me.

Now don't get me wrong, I am ecstatic to start my new college program in the Spring. I've just accepted that I will not be making a career out of working for Disney. In theory, I could apply to go full- or part-time within Merchandise or Attractions, but I miss Massachusetts, and don't like living in Florida enough to stay here for a job that isn't worthwhile to me. If I were to stay full or part time in another, more front line role, there would still be the opportunity for upward mobility in the company, just not in the timeframe that I would like.

While I'm tempted to point out the irony in working for a company dedicated to making dreams come true, only to be rejected for my dream role, I no longer feel that way. Working in Guest Relations was a dream. *Was.* My new dream is to build a career back in New England so I can afford a Disney Vacation Club Membership and an annual pass so that I can come back and enjoy the Disney magic as a *guest*.

I don't regret the Disney College Program. I was able to make dreams come true for others, and there is no other job where you'd be able to say that. I was there for lost children when they needed to be comforted with their parents nowhere to be found. I was one of many who retrieved lost wallets off the DINOSAUR ride and returned them to their grateful owners. I explained the history behind Epcot and Spaceship Earth to first-time guests who would have never expected that level of knowledge and passion from a lowly Merchandise Cast Member. I was able to congratulate Make-A-Wish kids for winning prizes on Comet Crasher, and to see the joy on their faces when I would give them the biggest plush turtles and sea serpents they'd ever seen. I saw first-hand the excitement that families experience together as they rush to ride Space Mountain early in the morning, and as they cry watching Wishes for the first time at night.

I've had the ability to experience these events, all while living right next to Walt Disney World, with people from all over the world, many of whom have become my best friends.

And that in itself is my dream come true.

Acknowledgments

Writing a book while simultaneously finishing up an undergraduate degree at St. Anselm College and working in the Disney College Program is no easy feat, and a number of "thank you's" are in order.

Thank you to my parents, grandparents, and the rest of my family, who supported me in what I wanted to do. This book would not have turned out the way it did without the support I had at home, and for that I am extremely thankful.

Thank you to Charlie (Chaz) who continued to support me in my pursuit of working for Disney, even after learning that we'd be spending five long months apart. And thank you for always being up for reading a new draft of the same chapters when I needed a second opinion.

Thank you to Amy Regan for supporting the idea of the college program and me writing a book about it, and for being my best friend since the SMS days.

Thank you to Theresa Colella, Paige McGowan, and Lindsay Fleming for keeping me sane during the last two years of college through all of the DCP applications and early book drafts. And thank you for making our S4 pod one of the best places in which to live and work on my resume in preparation for Disney.

Thank you to Holly Lewis, Paulina Genovese, and Lexie Athanas for being awesome roommates during the DCP and not making fun of my Dino-Rama costume every time I walked into the living room wearing it.

Thank you to Aroha Tamatea, Anthony Quiterio, Abbi Smith, Cleo McClintock, Kylie Semler, Kaori Takahashi, Misaki Yokochi, Joshua Emil, Rayme McKelvey, Devin Scott, Nikki Ogilvie, Cristian Perez, Nora Marimon, Natalie Bermudez, Caitlin Hill, Kate Adams, Aly Schmidt, Anthony Figueroa, Rachal Layne, Jessica Marie, Tyler Fritz, Jamie Grace, and Taylor Davis, and the rest of my DAK/DCP friends for making my Disney experience truly unforgettable.

Special thank you to Joshua Torres for making my first experience on Tower of Terror the best it could have possibly been, despite the possible lack of circulation in his arm.

Thank you to Kaitie Smith and Sara Loretta, who although were not physically on the DCP with me were there in spirit, and who continue to be inspirations for me.

Thank to St. Anselm College, for improving my writing skills over the past four years.

Thank you to Walt Disney, for his amazing creativity and hard work overcoming obstacles to eventually found what is presently one of the greatest companies in the world to work for.

Thank you to all my Instagram, Facebook, and Blogger followers for keeping me motivated to keep writing.

About the Author

Brittany Dicologero is a recent graduate of St. Anselm College, in Manchester, NH, where she earned her bachelor of arts degree in history. She completed two Disney College Programs, one in Dinoland U.S.A., in Merchandise, and one at Lights, Motors, Action! Extreme Stunt Show and Fantasmic!, in Attractions.

Brittany Earns Her Ears is her first book, and she also writes for the websites DisneyQuestions.com and DisneyFanatic.com.

Brittany resides in Saugus, MA, and plans to continue writing from the New England area.

About the Publisher

Theme Park Press is the largest independent publisher of Disney and Disney-related pop culture books in the world.

Established in November 2012 by Bob McLain, Theme Park Press has released best-selling print and digital books about such topics as Disney films and animation, the Disney theme parks, Disney historical and cultural studies, park touring guides, autobiographies, fiction, and more.

For our complete catalog and a list of forthcoming titles, please visit:

ThemeParkPress.com

or contact the publisher at: bob@themeparkpress.com

. . . .

Theme Park Press Newsletter

For a free, occasional email newsletter to keep you posted on new book releases, new author signings, and other events, as well as contests and exclusive excerpts and supplemental content, send email to:

theband@themeparkpress.com

or sign up at www.themeparkpress.com

. . . .

More Books from Theme Park Press

Amber Earns Her Ears

My Boss, Mickey Mouse

Come read Amber Sewell's Disney College Program diary and share her successes and her failures, her moments of delight and her moments of despair, and learn what happens when the pixie dust settles and the guests have gone home.

ThemeParkPress.com/books/ amber-earns-her-ears.htm

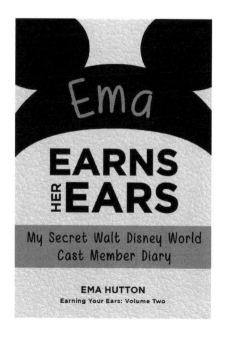

Ema Earns Her Ears

God Save the Mouse!

Ema Hutton's two summers in Disney's International College Program took her from a little town in England to cleaning rooms at Port Orleans and performing as Pluto in the Magic Kingdom. Ema gives the most revealing glimpse yet of working backstage at Disney World.

ThemeParkPress.com/books/ ema-earns-her-ears.htm

More Books from Theme Park Press

Sara Earns Her Ears

From Cali to the Castle

For California girl Sara Lopes, it wasn't enough to walk down Walt Disney World's Main Street. She wanted to "live" there. She got her wish, for a little while, and her secret cast member diary takes you with her from Cali to Cinderella Castle.

ThemeParkPress.com/books/ sara-earns-her-ears.htm

Katie Earns Her Ears

From Texas to Tomorrowland

In this Disney College Program diary, Texas girl Katie Hudson leaves behind her small town for a new life in Walt Disney World's Tomorrowland, experiences rogue roommate drama you won't believe, and realizes that most pixie dust is bittersweet.

ThemeParkPress.com/books/ katie-earns-her-ears.htm

More Books from Theme Park Press

The Ride Delegate

Disney World for the 1%

The rich and famous experience Disney World differently from the rest of us: they're escorted by VIP Tour Guides, elite Cast Members who truly do hold the keys to the kingdom. Come meet the eccentric, outrageous guests who turned former VIP Tour Guide Annie Salisbury's life into a reality show.

ThemeParkPress.com/ books/ride-delegate.htm

Two Girls and a Mouse Tale

Double Shot of the Disney College Program

Two girls from Colorado spend a year in the College Program at Walt Disney World, balancing pixie dust with reality bites, as they spin magic for guests in the parks, but can't talk their roommates into keeping the apartment clean.

ThemeParkPress.com/books/ two-girls-mouse-tale.htm

Discover our many other popular titles at:

www.ThemeParkPress.com

Made in the USA
Middletown, DE
26 June 2015